HE TOUCHED ME

OTHER BOOKS BY BENNY HINN

The Anointing

The Biblical Road to Blessing

Good Morning, Holy Spirit

Kathryn Kuhlman:
Her Spiritual Legacy and Its Impact on My Life

Welcome, Holy Spirit

HE TOUCHED ME

An Autobiography

Benny Hinn

THOMAS NELSON PUBLISHERS®
Nashville

Published in Nashville, Tennessee, by Thomas Nelson, Inc.

The Bible version used in this publication is THE NEW KING JAMES VERSION. Copyright © 1979, 1980, 1982, Thomas Nelson, Inc., Publishers.

The photographs that appear in this book are the property of Benny Hinn and Benny Hinn Ministries and are used by permission.

ISBN 0-7852-6600-3 (PB edition)
ISBN 0-7852-7887-7 (HC)
ISBN 0-7852-6867-7 (FL edition).

Printed in the United States of America.

5 6 7 8 9 10 PHX 04 03 02 01

This book is dedicated to my wonderful Lord and Master, Jesus, God's Holy Son, who has done great things. To Him belongs all the glory, now and evermore. I want to thank Him for my dear father, Costandi Hinn, and mother, Clemence, whom I love with all my heart.

Contents

CHAPTER 1

WAR CLOUDS OVER JAFFA

"Benny, I need you to help me," said my beloved yet stern father, Costandi, handing me a shovel. There was a tense, uneasy tone in his voice.

This was not an idle request from a dad to his fourteen-year-old son. It was an order—and I knew exactly why he needed my help.

Immediately, we began to dig a deep trench in the garden of our home at 58 Ibn Rashad in Jaffa, Israel—the historic port city on the southern edge of modern Tel Aviv. "I really hope this won't be necessary," my dad lamented, "but we'd better be prepared. Who knows what will happen? Who knows?"

After toiling several hours in the hot Middle Eastern sun, the trench was deep enough. It could provide refuge for the entire Hinn household—plus room for a few neighbors who might need shelter. Earlier that same week, at College de Freres, the French-Catholic school I attended, there was an air-raid drill and we were herded into an underground bunker.

Inside our home, my mother, Clemence, and my older sister, Rose, were storing food and bottles of water. They were giving last-minute instructions to my younger brothers and sister. Up and down the street, people were painting the headlights of the cars black—and covering the windows of their homes.

It was the first week of June 1967. Night after night our family listened intently to Radio Cairo in our native Arabic language and we knew that war was imminent. Just a few days earlier, Egypt's President Nasser announced that the entire Egyptian army was to be on full alert. In a well-publicized demonstration, he moved large numbers of forces through the streets of Cairo en route to the Sinai. In some quarters, this was to be the battle to end all battles—threatening to once and for all crush the nineteen-year-old state of Israel and drive it into the sea.

Nasser was at the peak of popularity, and it seemed that hysteria had seized the entire Arab world. Jordan, Syria, and Lebanon had joined in an alliance for this historic confrontation, plus contingents from Saudi Arabia, Kuwait, Iraq, and Algeria had pledged to join the fray.

In Jaffa, the people were terrified. Israel was ringed by 250,000 Arab troops—including 100,000 Egyptian soldiers in the Sinai. There were 2,000 tanks and more than 700 bomber and fighter aircraft—far outnumbering the forces of Israel.

"Why?" I asked again and again. "Why is this happening? Why do people want to fight?" I didn't understand.

The hatred and emotional bitterness that suddenly rose to the surface in our community were shocking to me. Until this moment I did not know the deep-rooted animosity that existed between Arabs and Jews.

In our home things were different. Yes, we considered ourselves Palestinians, yet our doors were always open to people from all quarters. My father worked for the Israeli government, and we counted among our close friends Muslims, Jews, and Christians. Religiously we were Greek Orthodox, yet I attended a school run by Catholic nuns.

Now, with the looming clouds of war, we were feeling the pressure to take sides—and I didn't like it. "Oh, if we could just leave this place," I told my parents. "Anywhere would be better than this!"

EGYPTIANS, ROMANS, AND TURKS

Jaffa was the only home I had ever known. In the 1960s it was a bustling, mostly Arab community on the Mediterranean Sea with a great yet troubled history. Every day I walked to school down Yefet Street. *Yefet* is the Hebrew word for Japheth—Noah's third son—who is credited with establishing the city after the Flood.

My brothers and I often played on the docks where Jonah boarded the ill-fated ship for Tarshish. Just a few feet away is the house of Simon the Tanner, where Peter was staying when the Lord instructed him to preach to the Gentiles.

Joppa (Jaffa) was a Canaanite city in the tribute lists of Pharaoh Thutmose in the fifteenth century B.C., even before Joshua fought the Battle of Jericho. And it was where the Phoenician king Hiram of Tyre unloaded cedar logs for King Solomon's temple.

The winds of war had not been kind to my birthplace. Jaffa was invaded, captured, destroyed, and rebuilt again and again. Simon the Vespasian, the Mamluks, Napoleon, and Allenby have all claimed her. This strategic port has been ruled by the Phoenicians, Egyptians, Philistines, Romans, Arabs, Muslims, and Turks. The British took control in 1922 until it became part of the new state of Israel in 1948.

Jaffa was—and still is—an international melting pot. Take a

walk near the landmark Jubilee Clock Tower, built by the Ottomans in 1901, and you'll hear locals conversing in French, Bulgarian, Arabic, Hebrew, and other languages.

During my childhood, the hundred thousand people of Jaffa had become engulfed by the exploding population of Tel Aviv to the north. Today, the metropolis has the official name of Tel Aviv-Jaffa. More than four hundred thousand call the area home.

The sounds, the sights, and the smells of this city can never be erased from my memory. Every time I make a pilgrimage, I head straight for an open-air bakery, Said Abou Elafia & Sons on Yefet Street. Nothing about this place has changed. They still make their famous Arabic version of pizza, with eggs baked on pita bread. The style has caught on, and now you see similar eateries all over Israel. This was Jaffa's first bakery in 1880 and is still run by the same family (four generations later). I become nostalgic just thinking about their bagels, za'atar breads (a delicious Middle Eastern spice concoction baked with olive oil), and cheese- or potato-filled zambuska. Oh, they are good!

"THE MERCIFUL ONE"

Because of my father's unique position in the community, the people of Jaffa seemed like an extended family—regardless of their social, ethnic, political, or religious persuasion. The area was a district of Tel Aviv, and my father, Costandi Hinn, can best be described as a liaison between the community and the Israeli government. He was an imposing man, six feet two inches tall, with a soft yet powerful personality. And he was perfect for the task.

The majority of my father's time was spent settling grievances between citizens and government agencies—plus finding employment for those in need. He had offices in Jaffa and Tel Aviv, yet there seemed to be a never-ending stream of people coming to our home with special requests. He did not turn them away.

My father's giving nature was not a pretense. It was part of a cherished legacy handed down for generations. Immediately following World War I, my dad's great-grandfather and his family—the Costandis—emigrated from their native Greece to Alexandria, Egypt. They saw a bright future in trade and commerce. One of his sons (my father's grandfather) became involved in providing food and clothing for those in poverty, and the people would say, "Let's go to El Hanoun"—which in Arabic means "the merciful one," or "the gracious one." Later, many began to call him "Hinn"—and the name caught on.

Since that's what the people called him, and he was now living in an Arabic culture, the decision was made to change his last name from Costandi to Hinn. I am thankful that the same spirit of generosity remains in our family to this day. (I recently learned that some of my relatives who remained in Egypt chose to return to the Costandi family name.)

Later, one of the Hinn sons (my grandfather) moved from Egypt to Palestine and settled in the thriving Arab community of Jaffa. When he married and had a boy, he called him Costandi—to honor the Greek family name.

Over the years, my mother has shared glimpses of her early life. Recently, with a twinkle in her eye, she related how she met and fell in love with my father.

Although my mother was born in Palestine, her mother's

family emigrated from the impoverished southern European nation of Armenia to Beirut, Lebanon, many years earlier. Her father, Salem Salameh, was a Palestinian.

After a typical arranged marriage when she was just sixteen years old, the couple settled in Jaffa—and among their children was a lovely daughter named Clemence.

My grandfather was a carpenter and also worked as an inspector in the orange groves.

BREAKING TRADITION

As a young man, Costandi Hinn lived in a Palestine that was governed by Great Britain. He served in the British army from 1942 to 1944, and later moved to Haifa—about sixty miles up the coast—where he found work in the port's customs office.

Separated from his family, in a city where he was a stranger, his social life practically came to a halt. "But I don't know anyone," he confided to his father when they discussed asking for a girl's hand in marriage.

When Costandi came home for a visit, one of his aunts told him about a beautiful Armenian girl. "Her name is Clemence," she told him. "And her family is also Greek Orthodox." That fact was extremely important.

"Too young for me," exclaimed Costandi, when he learned she was only fourteen years of age.

However, when a meeting was finally arranged between the Hinn and Salameh families, my father quickly changed his mind. He said to himself, "She is lovely. This is the girl who will be my wife."

Not many days later, he went to the restaurant owned by Mr.

Salameh and asked if he could speak privately with him. A very nervous Costandi said, "Sir, I have a request. I want something from you."

Because of the respect that existed between the two families, he answered, "Whatever you want. I'll give it to you." He smiled and said, "Do you want my eyes?"

"No," replied Costandi, "I want your daughter, Clemence."

Mr. Salameh did not hesitate. "Yes," he replied. "I am very pleased. If that is your wish, she will be yours."

Yet, when the word quickly spread of what had taken place, there was great consternation. "That's not the way it is done!" shouted one agitated grandmother. "Why didn't his father come and ask for her hand the proper way? A young man doesn't go to a restaurant and ask such a question by himself!"

According to custom in the Middle East—even to this day—marriages are to be arranged between parents. So, to honor tradition, the elder Hinns made the request personally, and soon everyone was smiling.

Costandi bought a gold ring and proudly placed it on the finger of Clemence. Unfortunately, their plans for marriage were about to be shattered by forces that would shake the very foundation of Palestine.

TORN APART

It was April 1948, and the tension in Jaffa had spilled into the streets. Cars were being firebombed. Stores were being looted. Snipers lurked on the rooftops. Night after night the rioting was out of control.

Since 1922, Palestine had been operated as a British mandate, yet now that was about to drastically change. It was announced that on May 15 the British—along with 100,000 British troops holding a fragile peace—would be leaving. The new state of Israel was about to be born, officially endorsed by the world community.

Since the end of World War II, hundreds of thousands of Jewish refugees had disembarked at Jaffa and Haifa, returning to their ancient homeland. The panic that spread through the Arab world was unprecedented. In Jaffa alone, the Arab population plummeted from 70,000 to just over 4,000. Families abandoned their homes and fled to Egypt, Jordan, Syria, and Lebanon.

The Salameh family grabbed their belongings and hurriedly left for Ramallah, a city just north of Jerusalem. The Hinns, unsure of the future, chose to remain in Jaffa. Clemence and Costandi were now separated by more than miles. There was an armed border between them that was illegal to cross.

On May 9, 1948, after a complete breakdown of municipal services, the remaining leaders of Jaffa issued a proclamation declaring it "an open city"—an undefended town. There would be no more fighting. The community would submit to Jewish rule.

Costandi was able to secure employment at the postal service in Jaffa, yet his heart was in Ramallah. "All I could think about was finding a way to see Clemence," he said. He spent days plotting and scheming—determined to somehow bridge that border and return with the girl he so deeply loved.

In 1949, Costandi told the family that he was taking a leave of absence from his work, and would secretly make his way to Ramallah. Without much notice, he journeyed at night along the coastline to the city of Gaza. There he secured passage on a boat headed for Egypt, and traveled incognito by bus to Jordan.

The reunion with Clemence was well worth the risk, yet the greatest barrier was still ahead. How would he legally bring her home? When and how would they marry? What documents would be necessary to make the marriage legal?

"Your father stayed for a long period of time," my mother told me. "And we talked about how we could return to Jaffa." During this period, Costandi found work with the Red Cross in Amman.

Amal, the mother of Clemence, had an idea. "Why don't you have two marriages? One here in Ramallah so you will have documentation, and the other in Jaffa so it will be recognized by the Israelis?"

The plan worked, and, with great relief to the couple, the guards at the border nodded their approval and allowed Costandi and his sixteen-year-old bride to enter the country and return to Jaffa.

"PLEASE, LORD!"

Now under Israeli rule, Jaffa's major industry, the citrus export business, once again began to thrive. "Jaffa Oranges"—large and succulent—were (and still are) in high demand throughout Europe. The word *Jaffa* stamped on an orange simply meant it was grown in Israel and shipped through the Jaffa port. Costandi, who knew most of the people in charge, was quickly hired as an inspector.

For Clemence, her life centered around her devotion to her husband—and to the Greek Orthodox Church. Yet there was something that deeply troubled her.

In December 1952, Clemence was at the St. Louis French

Hospital on Yefet Street, about to give birth to her second child.

From her room, the third window from the corner of this historic 1883 building, she gazed at the deep blue waters of the Mediterranean. It seemed to stretch to infinity.

In the distance she could see a black cluster of rocks—the Andromeda rocks. According to Greek legend, the maiden Andromeda was chained to one of them when Perseus flew down on his winged horse, slew the sea monster, and rescued her.

Now Clemence wished someone could swoop down and save her from one more year of humiliation and disgrace. Even though she was devoutly religious, she didn't know about having a personal relationship with the Lord. Yet in that humble hospital room, in her own way, she made a bargain with God.

She walked over to the window, looked up into the sky, and spoke from the depths of her being: "God, I have only one request. If You'll give me a boy, I'll give him back to You."

Again, she repeated her cry. "Please, Lord. If You'll give me a boy, I will give him back to You."

"I SAW SIX LILIES"

You must understand the culture of the Middle East to realize the dilemma she faced.

The first child born to Costandi and Clemence Hinn was a beautiful girl, named Rose. Yet in the Hinn ancestral tradition, the firstborn should have been a son and heir.

She could hear the biting words from some of the Hinn family ringing in her ears. They chided her for her failure to produce a boy. "After all," one of them told her, "each of your other sister-in-laws had boys." The jeering and mocking often reduced her to tears. She felt embarrassment and shame. That night, on her hospital bed, her eyes were moist as she fell asleep.

The next day, however, her wish was granted. On Wednesday, December 3, 1952, at 2:00 P.M., I was born.

When I was young, my mother told me about a dream she had just after my birth. I thought it concerned a bouquet of roses, but recently she explained it was about lilies.

"I saw six lilies—six beautiful lilies in my hand," she said. "And I saw Jesus enter my room. He came to me and asked me for one of them. And I gave Him one lily."

When she awakened, Clemence asked herself, What does this dream mean? What can it be?

Eventually, our family was to have six boys and two girls, yet my mother never forgot her bargain with God. "Benny," she said, "you were the lily I presented to Jesus."

CHAPTER 2

A BOY NAMED TOUFIK

It is the custom of Greek Orthodox families to give a child one name at birth and a Christian name—usually after a saint or a priest—when they are baptized into the church. Since I was the first son, I was proudly named after my dad's father, Toufik. Almost immediately, my aunts, uncles, and cousins began calling me "Tou Tou."

My baptism took place at the residence of the Greek Orthodox priest in the historic area of Jaffa known as the Old City. Officiating was Benedictus, a friend of our family who became the patriarch of Jerusalem. Not only did he anoint me with oil and water—but I was also given his name. Now it was official: I was Toufik Benedictus Hinn. Later, I would simply be called "Benny."

The only house I knew in Jaffa once belonged to a family who fled Palestine when the city was practically deserted during the bloodshed of 1948. They left in great haste, and possession of the imposing three-story structure was given to the Greek Orthodox Church. My father was overjoyed when the local priest asked, "Mr. Hinn, would you consider moving your family into this residence?" We would occupy only one level of the house, but there was ample room.

The location was wonderful. It was situated on a high bluff, just two blocks from the blue waters of the Mediterranean, yet only a short walk to the heart of the community.

What an active place it became. The top floor of the building was given to the treasurer of the church, the second story became the Greek Orthodox Club, a gathering place for organizations of the church, and our home was located on the ground floor.

The imposing beige and rust structure had beautiful columns with wide stairs leading to the second level. In the courtyard sat a fountain stocked with tropical fish. Behind the house was a large garden with blooming citrus trees and flowers—and a walkway that led to the beach.

On the facade of the building was the insignia of the Greek Orthodox Club—an organization my father was president of for several years.

Our home had a spacious family room and two large bedrooms—one for my parents and the other for the growing household. First there was Rose, then me, followed by my brothers, Chris, Willie, Henry, and Sammy, and another sister, Mary. By the time I was a teen, our bedroom in Jaffa began to resemble a hospital ward. The eighth child, Michael, was born later in Canada.

Situated at the back of the house, on a raised level, was the kitchen. That's where I spent a great amount of time as a child— helping my mother prepare food. What was my favorite task? Making pita bread. I learned how to mix just the right amount of water, dough, and yeast. My mother used to brag, "Benny makes the best bread in town." They even used it on occasion for communion at our church.

"TAKE THIS. IT'S YOURS!"

My father's involvement in social work extended far beyond office hours. He was extremely gracious to people and there was a steady stream of local people visiting our home—especially those looking for work. Part of my father's duties as a government liaison to the community was to authorize the paperwork for laborers. For example, a hospital would say, "We need ten workers immediately." So my father would interview the prospects and make the choices.

In the back of the garden he stored huge bags of flour he constantly purchased. When someone was in need, he would say, "Here, take this flour with you. It's yours!"

My mother, a wonderful Middle Eastern cook, added to the hospitality. "Why don't you stay for something to eat?" she would tell them.

On Saturdays and Sundays our house was overflowing. We would use the ovens of a bakery about 400 feet from our house to bake bread from the dough we had mixed at home. My brothers would help me as we put the dough in big round dishes on our heads and walked to the bakery every weekend. While they were playing, I'd sit there and watch the bread rise, calling them when it was ready.

Our dining table was a picture of abundance. There were always a dozen dishes—stuffed squash, rice wrapped with grape leaves, spicy foods and hummus—a puree of chickpeas. For dessert there were sweets, such as baklava, a delicate layered pastry dripping with honey.

Perhaps the reason I eat very little meat today is because it was not served in great quantities in our home and I didn't develop a taste for it. Even now I much prefer dishes made with vegetables and rice.

"MY CHILDREN, MY WEALTH"

When I tell people about my father's generosity, they say, "Oh, he must have been such a joy to be around."

To be candid, my dad's personality put the fear of God in me and my brothers and sisters, yet we loved him deeply.

When the visitors were gone, and only our family was at the table, we would eat quickly and quietly. There were no family discussions at mealtime and I knew practically nothing about my father's work until I was a teenager. We never talked about money, politics, or major issues.

One matter, however, was clearly understood. If we talked at the table we were in trouble. And if we were really mischievous he would give us a spanking on the spot—with a stick.

We knew that my father's occupation involved a great amount of pressure.

When he came home from work he always took a short nap and we knew better than to wake him. I can still remember the day a distraught woman came looking for my dad. "No, I'm sorry, you can't see him. He's sleeping," one of my bothers insisted.

Paying no attention, the woman barged right in, brushed us aside and walked into his bedroom, waking him with a stick she was carrying. Oh, what a commotion that caused. A few seconds later the woman was running out the front door—and my dad was chasing her with her own stick! Then the tables turned! We were all in deep trouble for allowing the woman to enter the house.

Mom was never the disciplinarian in our home. It wasn't necessary. My father dished out all that was required—and perhaps a little more. One day he came home to find Chris and I fighting. "Chris, come over here," my dad demanded. "He put his feet on the toes of my brother, looked him in the eyes and gave Chris a stern scolding. Then he did the same to me.

Despite his strict ways, we were all vying for my father's attention. The smallest act of kindness from him meant the world.

I recall the time he took a business trip to Cyprus when I was about six years old. He brought back a toy gun for me to play with. It was about twelve inches long and sparks would shoot from it every time you pulled the trigger. Two days later, when my brother Chris took the little gun from me and broke it, I thought I would never stop crying. This was no ordinary toy. It was one of my most cherished possessions—because it was from my dad.

On the outside, my father's shell was harder than a tortoise, but I never doubted his love for me. Rarely would he pay us a personal compliment, yet he would say the most glowing things about us to my mother—and she could not keep it a secret.

Once, when a neighbor said, "Costandi, you must be proud of your children," he replied, "My children are my wealth. I'm not a millionaire, but I have a wonderful family who are all healthy. I am blessed."

My mother and father never openly displayed any of the affection they shared between each other. I can't even remember seeing my parents holding hands. It just wasn't done! Yet we could feel the depth of their love.

HERCULES, TARZAN, AND THE LONE RANGER

Saturday! Oh, we couldn't wait for Saturday. As sure as the sun would rise, Mom would be in the kitchen making sandwiches and lemonade for us to take to the beach. Although the sea was only a stone's throw from our home, we loved the beach at Bat Yam, a forty-five-minute walk south of Jaffa. Dad always went with us—and there were usually a few cousins tagging along.

We thought nothing of walking that distance. We walked everywhere. My father didn't own an automobile the entire time we lived in Israel—he either walked to work or took public transportation.

We could always depend on the weather. People are surprised to learn that rarely does a drop of rain fall on Israel from May through November.

I liked the water, but not the rough-and-tumble play of some of my brothers. I preferred to stay a few paces away from the crowd. Some people thought I was a loner. Actually, I didn't particularly like the idea of drowning!

If it was windy we would fly kites on the beach—running as fast as our legs could carry us.

In the afternoon we'd rush back home, eat some corn-on-the-cob and walk upstairs to the Greek Orthodox Club to watch the weekly movies for kids. Laurel and Hardy. Hercules. Tarzan. The Lone Ranger. Dad was the projectionist and we saw them all—in English with no subtitles.

Glued to the screen, I'd watch those movies and dream of leaving Israel and moving to the West. "That's me," I would say to myself. "There I am right there!"

When we played cowboys and Indians in the yard, I always pretended I was an American, and bragged about my knowledge of the United States—even though it was limited to what I had seen on the screen.

Since I was small for my age, the boys in the neighborhood thought they had someone to pick on. Sure, I could defend myself, but rarely was it necessary. My brothers watched over me like eagles. Once when a Greek boy hit me, my brother Chris jumped in and began pounding the kid with his fists. When it was over, the boy was taken to the hospital with a broken arm. Oh, was Chris in trouble!

I WAS SHUNNED

I wish I could tell you that my childhood in Jaffa was perfect and without trauma. That is not the case. From the age of three, my self-image was so shattered that I continually wanted to run and hide. The humiliation and shame I experienced began with a horrible stuttering problem that surfaced when I was sent to preschool. As members of my family will tell you, it took what seemed forever for me to complete one simple sentence.

My speech was so halting that my teachers, precious Catholic nuns, avoided asking me questions in class—attempting to spare me from embarrassment. At playtime I was shunned. The boys and girls didn't want to talk to me because I had such a difficult time responding. As a result I had few friends.

By the time I reached my fifth birthday I began withdrawing from anyone who came near. Many nights I buried my head in my pillow and cried myself to sleep. When people came to visit our home I would run to my room and crawl under the bed, hoping no one would find me. I thought, *If they hear me they're just going to make fun of my stuttering.*

Chris, my younger brother, was keenly aware of my problem and became both my protector and my spokesman. Often, when someone would ask me a question, Chris would answer before I had the chance to say a word.

People can be cruel to someone with a handicap. Even those who loved me said, "Benny, with your speech problem, you probably won't amount to much in life." Those words, repeated in so many subtle ways, became indelibly etched on my young mind.

My mother once sent me to a neighbor's home to give the woman something she had requested. I haven't a clue what I took, but I will never forget what was said. The woman looked at me and began to laugh. She remarked, "Why did your mother send someone who can't talk?"

One morning my father asked me to walk to a nearby house to pick up some birdseed. I was just five years old. When I arrived at the door of the house a man came out with the seed and spoke words that affected me deeply. He said, "Why do you look so dumb?"

My self-worth had already been devalued, and now I was being told I appeared to be "dumb." Dejected, I went away thinking, *He said I looked dumb, so I must be!*

Peter Bahou, the boy who lived next door, was concerned about my problem. We would sit together on the front steps and he would hand me a book. "Benny, I'd like you to read to me." Some days my stuttering was so severe he would have to calm me down. "It's okay," Peter assured me, "you don't have to do it now. We can read later."

FATHER HENRY

My formal education began at the Catholic Nuns' School. To this day I can close my eyes and picture my kindergarten teacher—a tall, thin, blue-eyed French nun who wore glasses. I don't recall anything specific she taught me, I only know how much she cared. "You are a very special young man," she would tell me. "You are very special." Oh, how I needed to hear those words.

On a recent trip to Jaffa, I asked the driver of our van to stop on Yefet Street in front of the College de Freres (School of Brothers), a Catholic institution built in 1882. It was my school from the first grade forward. There were 400 students when I attended—it has now grown to more than 900.

I opened the door to room 1-C, a classroom where I spent so many days, and little had changed. "Let me tell you about that blackboard," I told the friends who accompanied me. "If your name was ever written there, you were in deep trouble. No one was allowed to talk to you until your name was removed." It was an effective form of punishment. Fortunately, because of my quiet nature, my name didn't make the list.

To my delight, Father Henry Helou was present during our visit. He had been one of my earliest teachers and was still on the faculty of the school. After we exchanged greetings, he told us that he watches our television programs, which are broadcast in Israel. "I never thought Benny would be a speaker," he told those who gathered around. "I used to teach religion, and every student was asked questions, but I often skipped Benny to keep him from being embarrassed." And he added, "Now, when I see him on television, I say, 'Is he the same one?'"

I smile when I realize that I learned to stutter in several

languages. Lessons at the Catholic school were in French and Hebrew. Greek was spoken in our church—and often at home, since my father's heritage was Greek. The principal language of our family, however, was Arabic.

On school day afternoons, the minute we walked into the house, we immediately did our homework. There wasn't any choice. My dad hired a woman we laughingly called the "gestapo"— who was both a baby-sitter and a tutor. She looked over our shoulder to make certain our assignments were perfect.

Finally, when she told us that study time was over, we rushed to the television set to watch stations from Lebanon, Cyprus, or Egypt—mostly American cartoons or programs such as *Gunsmoke*.

A typical night after dinner would find Dad in the back of the house talking with friends, while Mom would sit on the front porch, catching up on the local gossip with women of the neighborhood. My brothers and sisters would usually watch another TV program before our eight o'clock bedtime.

In our room, we'd often fall asleep with our little radio tuned to Middle Eastern music coming from an Egyptian or Jordanian station. Some nights I'd read one of the books I checked out of the library—like the French language version of *Rin Tin Tin*.

School started promptly at 8:00 A.M., a twenty-minute walk from our house. Some days it took a little longer because I would stop at a store on the way to buy a donut with cream on the inside. Now that was a treat!

"DON'T TELL MOM!"

I loved my brothers and sisters, yet each personality was as different as chalk from cheese.

Rose was my older sister and I always looked up to her, yet as kids we had our squabbles. If I had a secret, she was the last person I'd tell—knowing she'd spread the news before sundown.

Christopher, one year my junior, was a card-carrying troublemaker. More than once he came home with a bloody nose, bragging, "I was only trying to protect you, Benny."

The gentleman who lived on the top floor of our house, Mr. Lutfalla Hanna, was kind to me, but not to Chris—and it was mutual. He used to park his car in the garage attached to the back of the house. And for a few days one summer, Chris took great delight in giving him two flat tires, making the poor man's life miserable. It abruptly stopped when Mr. Hanna told my father, "Keep your boy away from my car, or I don't know what I will do!"

Willie, next in line, was one of my favorite brothers. He was quiet and shy; always thinking, and an extremely hard worker. Who did I confide in? Willie. If there ever was a "Don't tell Mom about this" moment, I would whisper it to him.

Then came Henry—perhaps even more mischievous than Chris. We sometimes laughed at him for being a little clumsy—especially the day he ran into the Communion table at the Greek Orthodox church we attended and made quite a mess. Henry also had an active imagination and had us believing outlandish stories.

As children, my brothers and I loved to watch wrestling on television—and following the matches we tried a few moves on one another. Again, it was Chris who did most of the damage. However, I once broke Henry's finger—and one day little Willie had to be taken to the hospital with a broken arm.

Sammy was just a tot when we lived in Jaffa. I helped my mother look after him—and often changed his diaper. To this day he is still "my little brother."

Mary, my younger sister, was the last of the Hinns to be born in Israel. There was always something special about her. Those who were present when she was baptized into the Greek Orthodox Church still talk about the glow that came over her face.

My aunts and uncles were constantly bragging about my brothers and sisters—predicting for each of them great success. I was the one for whom they worried.

What will become of Benny? they wondered, thinking about my impediment.

Would this "heavy tongue" be a burden I would always carry?

CHAPTER 3

FIRE FROM ABOVE

"Benny, would you like to become an altar boy?" asked Father Gregorios, the priest at St. George's Church—the central Greek Orthodox church in Jaffa.

I was thrilled. After all, St. George's played a central role in my life, and its rich traditions were woven into the fabric of our family. What a colorful, beautiful edifice it was, decorated with religious icons and wall paintings.

From as early as I can recall, I was taught that by praying to the Virgin Mary and the saints, I was communicating with God. It was also the custom of church members to kiss the icons.

Father Gregorios taught us that liturgical worship is designed to appeal to all the senses—the worshipper's eyes see the beauty of the sacred paintings, his ears hear the age-old hymns, he smells the incense and tastes of the Communion. I was also instructed that our body is to glorify the Creator by symbolic gestures, and our spirit rises in adoration of the heavenly Father.

At the age of seven I said my confession, learned the Nicene Creed, and participated in the Eucharist. Then, as an altar boy, I wore special robes and assisted the priest during the service. Sometimes I would carry a candle or hold the incense. The service—called the Divine Liturgy—has not changed since the early days of Christianity.

It was always a special day when the priest would include me with church members who were invited to his residence for a meal. He was a cherished friend of our family.

My introduction to miracles took place at the site just outside Jaffa where Peter raised Tabitha from the dead. Once each year the entire Greek Orthodox community gathered at the spot for an all-day celebration and picnic.

At the special service the priest recounted the story from Scripture where Peter knelt next to the dead woman and prayed, "'Tabitha, arise.' And she opened her eyes, and when she saw Peter she sat up. Then he gave her his hand and lifted her up; and when he had called the saints and widows, he presented her alive. And it became known throughout all Joppa, and many believed on the Lord" (Acts 9:40–42).

A GREAT INFLUENCE

Because of the daily training in Catholic schools over many years, in my heart I also considered myself to be a Catholic. I attended Mass regularly and knew how to pray Hail Mary, the Nicene Creed, the Lord's Prayer, and other prescribed prayers.

The Catholic sisters had a great spiritual influence on me. At school they taught me the Scripture at a very young age. It was there I first learned about Abraham, Isaac, Jacob, and the miracles of Christ.

Did my parents protest? No. A private Catholic school education was considered to be the best available. Yet on Sunday I also felt comfortable being involved in the rituals of the Greek Orthodox Church.

During this time of intense religious instruction, I would

bring my specific requests to God, yet I did not know how to personally talk to the Lord. In reality, my prayer life was very organized—and very routine.

In many ways I feel blessed when I think about the spiritual training I received. I often think, *How many kids are taught the Old Testament in Hebrew? And how many young people get to take field trips that make God's Word literally come alive?*

I remember traveling into the Negev and being taught about Abraham—standing next to the well he had dug. That experience will never leave me.

A SPECIAL GIFT

Without question, seeds from heaven were being sown into my life.

Once, when I was about seven years old, a gentleman from Nazareth knocked on the door of our house. He was a born-again evangelical Christian—something I had no concept of at the time.

He gave me a very special gift—a small booklet that contained a portion of the Bible. It was illustrated with colorful drawings.

About two weeks later he returned with a second booklet. I had a big smile on my face as I said, "Thank you, sir."

Somehow, I was drawn to the booklets and was excited every time the man came to our door. I believe he knew that I was responding to the Scriptures, while others in the neighborhood showed little interest.

Anxious to receive the entire set of booklets, I asked, "Would you bring me all of the Bible?" On his next visit that's what the man from Nazareth gave me.

From the events of Jesus' life I had learned at school, I cut out the pictures from different booklets and put the life of Christ in order—making my own special volume.

To me, this was a treasure. I kept the book in my room for years and recounted the story of Christ again and again.

CLICK, CLICK, CLICK

In both the Greek Orthodox tradition and the Catholic church there is a strong emphasis on miracles and healing. My mother added Middle Eastern folk remedies to her belief, and often practiced these treatments on her children.

Once I was quite sick with a chest cold and my mother asked me to lie down on my stomach. She took small glass cups, placed alcohol-doused cotton balls in them, and lit them on fire.

One by one, she would place the cups on my back—about twenty of them. Since fire needs oxygen, the fire would immediately be extinguished and I could feel the suction—pulling the cold right out of me.

When she would pull off the cups, you could hear the *click, click, click.* "Look, Benny, here's your cold," my mother said, showing me how the burned cotton had become greenish.

This method of "sucking out a cold" is still practiced today.

I can also recall the time my mother had a disease that showed up as boil-like eruptions on her skin. Many of them began to bleed and the condition stayed for weeks.

My mother didn't know what to do until a woman showed up at our home and said, "Cover your body with fig leaves."

We laughed and thought the woman had lost her mind. My

mother, however, followed the advice, and the next morning the boils were gone. They never returned.

Years later, while I was reading the Old Testament, this Scripture jumped out at me: Hezekiah was suffering and Isaiah said, "Let them take a lump of figs, and apply it as a poultice on the boil, and he shall recover" (Isa. 38:21). Hezekiah was healed!

I LOOKED INTO HIS EYES

People have asked, "Benny, when did the Lord begin to move in your life?"

At the age of eleven, God spoke to me through a vision of the night—the only time anything like it occurred during my childhood in Jaffa. I can recall it as if it happened yesterday. I saw Jesus walk into my bedroom. He was wearing a robe that was whiter than white and a deep red mantle was draped over His shoulders.

I saw everything—His hair, His eyes. I saw the nail prints in His hands.

At this early time in my life I did not know Jesus. I had not asked Christ to come into my heart. Yet the moment I saw Him, I knew it was the Lord.

I was asleep when it happened, but suddenly my young body was caught up in an incredible sensation that can only be described as "electric." I felt charged, as if someone had plugged me into a wired socket. There was a numbness—as if a million needles were pricking my body.

At that moment, the Lord stood before me, and He looked at me with the most beautiful eyes. He smiled, and His arms were open wide. I could feel His presence—it was marvelous.

The Lord didn't say anything. He just looked at me, and then disappeared.

Almost instantly, I was wide awake, and could scarcely understand what was happening. God had allowed me to experience a vision that would create an indelible impression on my young life.

As I awakened, the wondrous sensation was still there. I opened my eyes and looked all around, but this intense power that I had never experienced before continued to surge through me. I felt totally paralyzed, and couldn't move a muscle. Yet I was in control. This unusual and indescribable feeling overtook me—yet didn't dominate me.

For the first time, Jesus touched my life.

The next morning I told my mother about the experience, and she still remembers her words to me. She responded, "Then you must be a saint."

Of course, I was certainly no "saint," but my mother believed that if Jesus came to me, He must be preparing me for a higher calling.

BRINGING THE HOLY FIRE!

Every year, the day before Easter, the churches of our area would choose five representatives to travel to Jerusalem on "Holy Fire Saturday." My father was always on that committee and I was asked by the priest to accompany the men.

The purpose of the journey was to bring back the Holy Light—a fire that is said to miraculously appear inside the tomb of Christ once each year to mark the Resurrection. It was a great honor, yet highly unusual that a young boy would be given this opportunity.

Leaving Jaffa early on Saturday morning, our first destination was the Greek Orthodox church in west Jerusalem. Representatives were there from every part of Israel.

It's important to understand that during those years, Israeli citizens could not journey to the Holy Sepulcher Church—the place of Jesus' tomb. This was prior to the 1967 Six Day War and the church was located in east Jerusalem, in territory that belonged to Jordan—still in a state of war with Israel at the time.

While we waited, the much-anticipated event was taking place. This was the day when fire from heaven is believed to suddenly appear in the Holy Sepulcher—just as it has for centuries.

When the patriarch and his entourage enter the basilica the crush of people is amazing. Perhaps you have seen the coverage of this celebration on national television. Thousand of worshippers are holding candles with great expectation. At noon the lights go out and the patriarch enters the tomb to wait for the Holy Light.

As the time draws near, people begin to chant in a loud voice, "Lord, have mercy! Lord, have mercy!"

Inside the sepulcher, at a certain moment, the Holy Light is said to supernaturally flash from deep inside the tomb. It lights a little lamp of olive oil placed near it. After reading prayers, the patriarch uses the lamp to light two clusters of thirty-three candles he is holding.

When he emerges from the tomb there is great rejoicing. Bells begin to ring, and the resurrection of Christ is celebrated by the passing of the fire—first to the official representatives of the Orthodox and Armenian churches, then to the assembled crowd.

The divine light is unusual. It is said to have a bluish hue, and at the first moments of its appearance, the priests say it will not burn their hands or face. Every year several pilgrims report seeing candles light up of their own accord.

At a specified time we would go to the military-guarded Mandelbaum Gate that separated east and west Jerusalem, waiting to have the Holy Fire passed from the other side. The moment was also special to my father and me because across the barbed-wire border was my uncle Michael, who always journeyed from Ramallah for the occasion.

In the distance, we could see the pilgrims coming toward us with their candles burning—ready to transfer the Holy Light to people who would carry the flame to their churches for Easter.

Every church had special oil lamps that would keep the light glowing the entire year. Then, just before Easter, they would extinguish the flame—waiting for the new light of the Resurrection.

On the road back to Jaffa people were waiting for us in town after town with their candles unlit—places like Remla and Lod. I felt honored. One of the men on the journey said, "Benny, you are the only boy in Israel who carries the Holy Fire to the churches."

When my father and I finally reached home after the events of the day, I was too excited to be tired. Plus, the next day was Easter.

To mark the special day, the Boy Scout troop to which I belonged led an annual parade from the Greek Orthodox Club (on the second level of our house), to St. George's Church.

We held banners and played trumpets and drums. From our home to the church, people lined the streets, waiting for our troop to pass by.

It was Easter! A time to celebrate.

My greatest thrill that day was not marching in a parade or waving a flag. In St. George's Church, I looked at the flickering light in the lamps of oil and said, "Thank You, Lord, for allowing me to carry the Holy Fire."

CHAPTER 4

THE TURMOIL

"How many days until we leave?" I anxiously asked my mother.

"It won't be long," she said, smiling. "You'll see your grandmother soon."

Although Grandma Amal lived less than two hours away, the heavily fortified border that separated Israel from the Arab nations was a barrier that divided our family. When my mother's family chose to flee from Jaffa to Jordan during the conflict in 1948, they didn't realize how permanent the isolation from their relatives would be.

During those years, the law strictly prohibited people from crossing back and forth—except for a three-day period at Christmas each year. The Jordanian government entered into a treaty with Israel permitting families to visit their relatives on the West Bank, but only at Christmastime.

"You have no idea how excited we were during our annual trip to your house in Ramallah," I told my mother's sister, Chafouah, recently.

"No, it wasn't just your family who was thrilled," she told me. "That was the highlight of our year—among our most cherished memories."

Since we didn't own a car, my father hired a taxi for the journey to the border. Unfortunately, that's as far as he could go.

Dad didn't make the complete trip with us to Ramallah, on the West Bank. "Mr. Hinn," his Israeli superiors told him, "because of your position with the government, we think it would be too dangerous for you to cross the border."

Since my father had many acquaintances at the checkpoint, they would walk us through without a problem.

Meeting us on the Jordanian side would usually be my uncle Michael, in his well-preserved Model-T Ford. He'd give us all big hugs and take us the rest of the way. Grandma's house was always packed with relatives—including Uncle Boutros and his family who arrived from Lebanon.

During my childhood, the holiday season was not about exchanging expensive gifts. It focused on being together with family. My aunts and uncles gave us coins at both Easter and Christmas and we would run to the store to buy ice cream and candy.

In Ramallah, there were plenty of special treats. Before my grandfather Salem passed away, he owned a small store that sold sandwiches and sweets. He would let us dip into the candy jars.

CHEERING RELATIVES

I loved my mother's family because they accepted me, despite my speech problems. Others made fun, but not the Salameh family.

At their house I became an extrovert.

"When are you going to put on the show?" my little cousins begged. They were talking about a skit, or a "production" I organized every year during our visit.

During those years there was a popular television comedy program in the region titled, *Doctor, Doctor, Follow Me!*

We did our own version of the show—complete with song-and-dance routines. You should have seen us—me, Willie, Chris, and our cousins entertaining a room full of cheering, exuberant relatives.

At Christmas, one of my uncles played "Papa Noel," handing out small toys and trinkets, and the story of Christ's birth was read.

During most years, we stayed in Ramallah for three days. And although our visits were brief, I still have many fond memories I cherish from those times.

IN THE GARBAGE!

It was impossible to live in Israel during the sixties without feeling the escalating political tension. Almost daily there were news reports of skirmishes along the border from Egypt to Lebanon.

Our house, in contrast to most families' in Jaffa, seemed like a small branch of the United Nations. On our porch and in our living room, you'd find Muslims, Christians, and Jews—conversing hour after hour.

One afternoon, when I was twelve, a general in the Israeli army who was a good friend of my father stopped by for a visit. He parked his jeep in front of the house.

Since our home was situated on a hill, he made sure the wheels turned toward the curb. Every time he'd come, my brothers and I jumped into the jeep and pretended we were in the army. This day, I was in the back with little Henry, Willie was up front and Chris was behind the wheel.

Somehow, Chris shifted the gears into neutral and straightened the wheels, and the vehicle began to roll backward. A neighbor saw what was happening and rushed over just in time to rescue Henry. Willie and Chris frantically jumped from the jeep, leaving me behind.

Just as the jeep was about to crash, I jumped into the neighborhood garbage dump at the bottom of the hill. The army vehicle flipped three or four times. It was totally demolished.

I don't even want to talk about the trouble we were in with my dad!

The army general, however, took the event in stride.

INTENSE PRESSURE

I thank God that I was brought up in a home that did not harbor hatred and resentment. My father often said, "Don't look at a situation from one side of the table. Always view it from four sides."

One evening he asked all the boys in the family to gather together. "Gentlemen," he began, "the forces in the Middle East will always be in conflict. Even if there is peace there will always be politics." He continued, "When I was born there were problems. I'm going to live through the problems, and when I die there will still be problems."

During the first several months of 1967, war was the number one discussion on the streets of Jaffa. Egypt was rattling its sabers and Iraq and Saudi Arabia pledged their solidarity with the Arab nations bordering Israel. The question of all-out conflict was no longer *if,* but *when.*

In our community, I could feel the intense pressure to take sides, and our family had no such plans. People knew we were

Greek Orthodox Christians and tested our loyalties. More than once my father was physically threatened for refusing to favor one faction over another.

At every turn I saw hatred rising to the surface and I thought, *Why can't we just leave—now!* My brothers and sisters felt the same. Anywhere would be fine—Belgium—Britain—it didn't matter. We wanted to escape this atmosphere of poison.

WHO IS WINNING?

I was at school on Monday morning, June 5, 1967, when the sirens began to wail. Immediately, we were all sent home.

We huddled around the radio, listening to the reports from Cairo. With military music playing in the background, the announcer declared, "Our forces are turning back the enemy on all fronts."

We looked at one another and said, "They must be close. They're going to show up any minute now." We were ready to jump into our carefully dug bunkers.

That night, neighbors came to our darkened house to listen to the reports from Egypt. The news was identical. Their army was moving across the Sinai and Israel was suffering massive defeats in the air, on land, and at sea. "Where are the planes?" we asked as we looked into the southern skies.

By the second and third days, if the reports from Cairo had been accurate, Israel's military would have been defeated three or four times over.

The Egyptians who broke the government order and listened to the British Broadcasting Corporation learned what was truly taking place.

Within the first few hours of Israel's Monday morning surprise air strike, most of Egypt's MiG-21s were destroyed while they were still on the ground. Nineteen Egyptian airfields were hit on the first day of war.

By the close of the second day, Israel had destroyed 416 Egyptian aircraft and Egypt's 100,000-man army was in full retreat. In one historic week, Israel captured all of the Sinai, the West Bank, and the Golan Heights, significantly expanding its boundaries.

Ramallah, the home of my mother's family, was the scene of an intense battle. When the bullets stopped flying, it no longer belonged to Jordan. It was now in Israeli hands.

"What has happened to my family?" my mother pleaded again and again. She was desperate for news.

One week after the war, I remember seeing my father dressed in Israeli army fatigues. His behavior seemed mysterious and he had little to say—and that night he did not come home.

However, the next day he returned with fantastic news. "Your family is fine," he announced proudly to my mother. He went on to tell her that the Israeli officers had provided the uniform and had personally taken him to Ramallah in the West Bank. I was deeply touched that my father had earned such respect and trust from the Israeli government.

Although his visit was brief, it was a great source of comfort to my mother.

"WE'RE MOVING"

I didn't realize it, but my father wanted to leave Israel before we as a family did.

About one year before the Six Day War, one of his Jewish

coworkers said, "Costandi, you really need to watch out for your family. You should seriously consider leaving."

For months, my father had spoken quietly with his Arab friends about the process involved in emigration. He was active in international service clubs and on a first-name basis with diplomats who lived in our area. Day after day, my dad was gathering valuable information that would affect the future of his family.

Early in 1968, my father called us together and announced he was making plans for us to leave the country. "Please don't discuss it with anyone because there may be some problems with our exit visas."

At one point he thought of moving to Belgium because we had some relatives there. I thought that would be great because I already knew the French language. Of course, I was ready to move *anywhere*.

A few days later, however, an attaché from the Canadian embassy came to our home and showed us a brief film on life in Canada. Toronto looked like an exciting city. Two of my father's brothers had moved to Canada, but we doubted they were financially qualified to become our official sponsors.

A BARGAIN WITH GOD

Oh, how I wanted to get away from the turmoil of the Middle East. One afternoon, alone, I got down on my knees—on that hard rock—and made a vow to God. "Lord, "I prayed, "if You will get us out, I'll bring You the biggest jar of olive oil I can find." And I added, "When we get to Toronto, I'll bring it to church and present it to You in thanksgiving."

At the time, bargaining with God didn't seem out of place. And olive oil was a precious commodity in the Greek Orthodox Church—used in the sanctuary oil lamps. So I made the vow.

About one week later, a man from the Canadian embassy phoned my father to say, "Mr. Hinn, we've worked everything out—don't ask me how. All of your paperwork is in order, and you can leave whenever you are ready."

Almost immediately, we sold our possessions and made preparations for a new life in North America.

We were not a wealthy family. The cost of flying to a new country and establishing a home was beyond our financial capability. Several miracles made the move to Canada possible. The Greek Orthodox Church put us in touch with agencies that helped sponsor our trip—funds we paid back after we were established in Toronto. Next, our neighbors, the Bahou family, were connected with a travel agency that assisted us with the tickets. Also, the Israeli officials my father worked with satisfied the government of Canada by certifying the trustworthiness of Costandi Hinn.

My father was in the prime of life, in his early forties, with a good, stable future—yet he put his family first. He sacrificed his future and gave up his dreams so that we could have ours.

During those last few days in the Holy Land my skin was tingling with excitement. I didn't know how or why, but I felt there was a great tomorrow waiting for me.

Jonah left the harbor of Jaffa and the result was the salvation of Nineveh. Peter heard the voice of God in Jaffa and he spread the message to Caesarea and to the ends of the earth.

I was just a boy. Yet, as the giant jet aircraft left the Tel Aviv airport, there was a lump in my throat. I wondered, *Will I ever see those wonderful Catholic nuns who so lovingly taught me? Will I ever meet Father Gregorios again?*

As the plane turned and we headed over the blue waters of the Mediterranean, I looked back and said one last farewell to the only home I had ever known.

CHAPTER 5

FROM THE KIOSK
TO THE CATACOMBS

When the Hinn family walked through customs in Toronto, there was no red carpet or brass band. We were immigrants, quietly entering a new land and facing an uncertain future. We arrived with the clothes on our backs, a few possessions in our suitcases, and a little money from what we had sold in Jaffa— enough to get by for a short time.

My father had no promise of a job and our housing was a small, rented apartment. What a shock to land suddenly in a "foreign" culture. I thought I knew a little English from watching American television programs as a child, yet it was intimidating to be totally surrounded by this new language.

My father, who spoke better English than any member of our family, filled out an employment application and landed a job selling insurance.

I will never know whether it was the pressure of raising a large family, or his self-confidence in meeting people, but my dad quickly became a success in his new occupation. Only a few months after arriving in Canada, we moved into our own home—on Crossbow Crescent in the North York section of Toronto, not far from the new Fairview Mall. We were all proud of our new surroundings.

Instead of Saturday walks to the beach, now there were Sunday picnics on the grassy slope of a nearby park. We were often joined by my father's two brothers—Elias and Raouf—and their families. Elias moved to Toronto via Belgium, and Raouf (with his wife and thirteen children) came to Canada directly from Jaffa. The men smoked and talked politics, the women gossiped, and we chased our cousins around the park.

At least once a month there was a big party at our home where everybody relaxed and danced to the familiar blare of Arabic music.

"YOU'RE HIRED!"

For the first time in my life I attended a public school—Georges Vanier Secondary School. And since most of the students my age had part-time jobs, that's what I wanted to do.

At the Fairview Mall there was a little kiosk that sold hot dogs and ice cream. Even though I had no previous work experience, the boss said, "You're hired!" So, that's where you could find me every day after school.

On my first payday, I took the small check home and, elated, showed it to my mom. "Look. This is for me. It has my name on it!"

The next Saturday I walked into a grocery store and asked the manager, "Where can I find the olive oil? I need the largest jug or container of it you have." He found what I was looking for.

On Sunday morning I proudly walked into the Greek Orthodox church and fulfilled the vow I had made to God in Jaffa. I placed the oil at the front of the altar and quietly said, "Thank You, Lord. Thank You for bringing us safely to our new home."

HAD BOB FLIPPED?

Because of my speech impediment, I wasn't much of a conversationalist at the kiosk—but I sure learned how to dish out the ice cream. The fellow I worked with was named Bob.

"What's this?" I asked him when I arrived at work one day in 1970. The booth looked weird. All over the walls he had tacked little strips of paper with verses from the Bible written on them. I thought, *This guy has flipped!*

Earlier, Bob had told me he was some kind of a Christian— far different from a Greek Orthodox. *Why all these Scripture verses?* I wondered. *Are they for me? I probably know the Bible better than he does!*

Curiosity got the better of me and I asked, "What's with the little pieces of paper?" That was the opening he was waiting for. Almost instantly, Bob began to tell me about Jesus—and how He died on the cross for my sin. I thought he would never stop; and when he finally did, I decided to stay as far away from this weirdo as I could.

It didn't work. Unless I quit my job, I'd have to be in that ice cream stand with him every afternoon.

Bob was relentless. Again and again he brought up the topic of religion—and even more—he continually talked about being "born again"—something that was not part of my view of Scripture.

I breathed a sigh of relief when Bob finally quit his job at the kiosk. Many of his "soul-winning" friends, however, attended my high school, and for the next two years I avoided them whenever possible. I thought, *What a bunch of kooks!*

Their view of religion seemed completely opposite of what I

had been taught by the Catholic nuns and Orthodox priest.

God, however, found a way to arrest my attention.

AN ENDLESS CHASM

During my senior year at Georges Vanier, for the second time in my life, I had an encounter with the Lord. It came in the form of an unforgettable dream.

In Jaffa, when I was eleven, the vision of Jesus standing before me made an indelible impression on me. However, now, in Toronto, my lifestyle was different. I was not involved in the study of Scripture. Yes, I still attended church, but what I was about to experience came as a surprise—totally unexpected.

Let me relate what happened in my bedroom on that chilly night in February 1972, when I was nineteen years old.

As the dream unfolded, I found myself walking down a long, dark stairway. The path was steep—so steep I thought I would fall. And it was leading me into a deep, endless chasm.

Even more, I was bound by a chain to a prisoner in front of me and to one behind. I was dressed in the clothing of a convict. Chains were shackled to my ankles and around my wrists. Then, as far as I could see ahead and behind me there was a never-ending line of captives.

The shaft was dimly lit, yet through the haze I watched dozens of small people moving around. I couldn't see their faces, and their bodies were barely visible. They looked like imps with strange-shaped ears—and we were being pulled down the stairs by them. It seemed as though we were a herd of cattle being taken to the slaughterhouse—or perhaps even worse.

Then, in a flash, the angel of the Lord appeared. It was a

glorious sight to behold. And the heavenly being hovered just ahead of me, only a few steps away.

What a sight! A bright and beautiful angel in the midst of that dark, forbidding hole.

Almost instantly, the angel looked into my eyes and motioned with his hand for me to join him. My eyes were riveted to his, and I began to walk toward him. Suddenly, the bonds fell from my hands and feet. No longer was I chained to my fellow prisoners.

The angel quickly led me through an open doorway and into a beautifully lit area. And the moment I stepped beyond the doorway, the heavenly being took me by the hand and dropped me on Don Mills Road—near the corner of Georges Vanier School. He left me just inches from the school wall, right beside a window.

Within one or two seconds, the angel disappeared.

I wondered, *What does all of this mean?*

CAN IT HURT?

The next morning I awoke early and rushed off to school before classes began. I needed to study in the library. I was seated at a large table, concentrating on my work, when a small group of students approached me. Immediately, I knew they were the same ones who had been giving me all this "Jesus talk."

"Would you like to join us in our morning prayer meeting?" one of them asked. They pointed to a room that was just off the library. I thought, *Well, perhaps I'll get them off my back if I agree. After all, one little prayer meeting isn't going to hurt me.*

"All right," I said as they walked with me toward the room. It wasn't a large group, only twelve or fifteen students. My chair, however, was right in the middle.

Suddenly, every member of the group raised their hands toward heaven and began to pray in languages I'd never heard before. My eyes became the size of saucers. These were students I had known in my classes—now talking to God with sounds I did not understand.

Until that time in my life I had never heard of speaking in tongues, and I was astonished. Here I was in a public school surrounded by a bunch of fanatics and I didn't comprehend it. All I could do was watch.

Then, one or two minutes later, something amazing occurred. Deep inside me swelled a sudden urge to pray—sadly, I didn't know what to say. Oh, every night I prayed to Mary, Joseph and all the saints, but "Hail Mary" did not seem appropriate for what I was feeling.

In my years of religious instruction I had never been taught the "sinner's prayer."

My mind flashed back to Bob in the kiosk, saying, "You've got to meet Jesus. You've got to meet Him!"

Meet Him? I thought I already knew Him.

"COME BACK"

I was uncomfortable. All around me were students lost in worship—yet no one was praying with me, or even *for* me. Without question, this was the most intense spiritual atmosphere I had ever encountered.

The idea that I was a sinner had never crossed my mind. I was a devout Catholic who prayed every night and confessed, whether I needed to or not.

In the middle of that room, I closed my eyes and spoke four words that changed my life forever. Out loud I said, "Lord Jesus, come back."

I had no idea why those were the only words that came out of my mouth. Again, I said, "Lord Jesus, come back."

What did it mean? Did I think Jesus had departed from my life? I had no answers. Yet the instant I uttered those words something came over me that took me back to the numbness I felt when I was eleven years old. It was not as intense, but I felt the voltage of that same force surging through me. Then I said to the Lord, "Come into my heart." And what a glorious moment that was!

His power was cleansing me from the inside out. I felt absolutely clean and pure.

Suddenly, in a moment of time, I saw Jesus. There He was. Jesus, the Son of God.

The students continued to pray—unaware of what was taking place in my life. Then, one by one, they began slipping out of the room, headed for their classes.

I looked at the clock. It was five minutes to eight o'clock in the morning. I sat there crying—not knowing what to say or do.

In that classroom, though I didn't fully comprehend it, Jesus became as real to me as the floor beneath my feet. My prayer had been so simple, yet I knew something extraordinary took place that Monday morning in February.

I rushed down the hallway—almost late for history class, one of my favorite subjects. That semester we were studying the Chinese Revolution. It could have been *any* revolution because that morning I didn't hear a word the teacher was saying. What had transpired a few minutes earlier would not leave me. When I closed my eyes—there was Jesus. When I opened them, He was still there. Nothing could erase the picture of the Lord's face I continued to see that day.

I'm sure some students wondered why I was wiping tears from my eyes. All I could say was, "Jesus, I love You! . . . Jesus, I love You!"

As I left school, I walked down the sidewalk to the corner and glanced at the window of the library. Instantly, everything began to fall into place—the angel, the dream—it all came tumbling back.

I wondered, *What is God trying to tell me? What is happening in my life?*

OPENING THE BOOK

In my bedroom was a big black Bible. I can't remember where it came from; it had been mine for years. In fact, it was the only Bible in our home.

I'm sure the pages hadn't been turned since our arrival in Canada, yet I was now drawn to it like a magnet. I sat on the edge of my bed, opened the sacred book and prayed, "Lord, You've got to show me what has happened today."

I turned to the New Testament—the Gospels—and began soaking up Scripture like a sponge. I didn't realize it then, but the Holy Spirit was becoming my teacher.

Those students at the prayer meeting did not rush up to me and say, "Now here's what the Bible says." In fact, they had no clue about what had occurred during the past twenty-four hours.

Then there were my parents. Fearing their reaction, I did not utter one word to my mother and father.

I had only been reading a few minutes when I found myself saying out loud again, "Jesus, I surrender all to You. Please, Lord Jesus, take all of me."

In every verse, the plan of salvation was being made real. I kept saying to myself, "I've never seen that before!" Or, "I didn't know that was in the Bible." The Scriptures came alive and began to take residence inside me.

The afternoon turned to evening, then to night. I didn't stop reading from that black Bible until three or four o'clock in the morning. Finally, I fell asleep—with a peace and assurance in my heart I had never known.

I could hardly wait for school to begin the next morning. The moment I spotted those "fanatics" I ran up and said, "Hey, I'd like you to take me to your church."

"Sure," they said with smiles on their faces. "Our fellowship meets every Thursday night and we know you'll love it."

AN UNUSUAL FLOCK

They called it "the Catacombs"—yet it certainly wasn't hidden, nor was it underground. I was totally unprepared for what I was about to experience with my newfound friends.

This was a church unlike any I had ever attended. When we walked into the sanctuary of St. Paul's Cathedral—an Anglican church in downtown Toronto—there were more than two thousand exuberant young people with their hands lifted toward heaven—praising God, singing and dancing before the Lord.

These were the days of the "Jesus People"—and the room was

full of born-again "hippies," who still hadn't cut their hair. They were jumping up and down—making a joyful noise unto the Lord. It was hard for me to believe that a place like this really existed. Yet somehow, from the very first night I felt at home. And, after what had transpired two days earlier, I, too, raised my hands and began worshiping God.

The shepherds of this most unusual flock were Merv and Merla Watson. Merv was a talented high school band director who had a life-changing experience through the Holy Spirit. Merla was a gifted songwriter and praise leader. Some of Merv's students asked if he would help them start a Christian club on campus. They decided to call it the "Catacombs Club," because they believed the times resembled the second days of the Roman Empire.

"We started with only six kids in a school of sixteen hundred," Merv later told me. "Then it grew to one hundred—three hundred—five hundred, and more." Watson became chairman of the Christian Performing Arts of Canada, which produced giant music festivals. The Catacombs kept growing—finally moving to St. Paul's to accommodate the crowds.

The service that night lasted more than three hours, yet it seemed like thirty minutes.

At the conclusion, Merv Watson announced, "I want all of you who would like to make a public confession of your sin to step forward. We are going to pray as you ask Christ to come into your heart."

I didn't understand much about God's power, yet inside I was tingling. Then I thought, *I don't think I should go down there because I'm already saved.* I was convinced that the Lord took control of my life at five minutes to eight on Monday morning. Now it was Thursday.

But somehow, I couldn't restrain myself. I began walking down that aisle as fast as I could. A voice inside was telling me, *Go up there.*

Here, in a charismatic service at an Anglican church, a professing Catholic from a Greek Orthodox home made a public confession of his acceptance of Christ. "Jesus," I said, "I'm asking You to be the Lord of my life."

Nothing in the Holy Land could compare with this. Jesus was not an icon, or a statue in a cathedral. He was alive and living in me—in Toronto!

All the way home I was smiling. The presence of the Lord was literally all over my being. I knew I would have to tell my mother what had happened to her nineteen-year-old son—I didn't have the courage to tell my father.

"Mama, I've got some good news for you," I whispered. "I've been saved."

In one split second her jaw was set. She glared at me and demanded to know, "Saved from *what?*"

"Trust me," I quietly replied. "You'll understand."

CHAPTER 6

WILL IT EVER END

It was unthinkable!

From the moment I awakened on Friday morning and for the rest of the day, a picture kept flashing before me. Everywhere I went—at school, at the kiosk, and that evening at home—I saw myself preaching.

I was not standing behind a pulpit in a neighborhood church. Instead, there were huge crowds of people gathered, and I was standing before them, wearing a suit. My hair was trimmed and neat and I was walking back and forth across the platform—boldly proclaiming the Word of God. It was a picture I could not shake.

That afternoon I saw Bob, the guy I had worked with at the Fairview Mall—who had once plastered the kiosk walls with Scripture. "You'll never believe what has happened to me this week," I began and quickly filled him in on the details of how I had found Jesus.

Then I shared the fact that I saw myself preaching. "Bob, all day long it's been like this. I can't erase the picture of me speaking in huge open-air rallies, in stadiums, in churches, in concert halls." I continued, "There are people as far as the eye can see. What do you think it means?"

I'm sure Bob must have wondered how I would ever be able

to stand before an audience and speak. His words, however, were totally encouraging. "There can only be one explanation," he told me. "God is preparing you for a great ministry. I think it's wonderful."

AN OUTSIDER

At home, the situation quickly deteriorated, turning from dreadful to disaster. From the moment of my conversion, my entire family began to harass and ridicule me. It was horrible.

I knew my father would be upset, but the reaction of my mother surprised me. She had always shown me such love and affection. How could her attitude change so quickly—and so drastically? Overnight, it seemed I was being treated as an outsider—someone who had betrayed the family.

My great offense was not in finding Christ, it was in breaking tradition. I doubt that the West will ever understand the thinking of Middle Easterners on this topic. It is treated as an unpardonable sin that brings humiliation to the family.

"Don't you realize you are dishonoring our reputation?" my father scolded. "Benny, you are ruining our family name."

Why did they feel such betrayal that I had become "born again"? As Greek Orthodox, they believe they are the *real* Christians—and they have the historical documentation to back them up, with a church dating back to the time of Christ.

I will always have a deep respect for those in the Greek Orthodox Church, and other Eastern "high church" orders. The honor they give to things that are sacred is beyond reproach. The problem, however, is one I was raised with. The faith is rich in dogma, form, and ritual, but impoverished when it comes to

God's presence or the anointing of the Holy Spirit. Everything I have seen tells me they are steeped in tradition, but they do not seem to understand the fullness of the Spirit.

What I had now discovered was a *personal* Christianity—a Jesus who was living in my heart. On that Monday morning at five minutes to eight, my life was transformed. It was something my family just could not comprehend.

From the firestorm that erupted I knew I had two choices: either stifle my conversation about Christ or be thrown out of my home. Nothing, however, could douse the flame that was now burning in my heart.

When I quietly told Chris, Willie, and Henry about my experience with Jesus, they ran to my father and said, "Dad, this country is making Benny nuts!" Then, when I added I was being called to preach the gospel, that was even worse. "First, you can't speak English," they chided me. "And second—you can't speak at all!" They laughed uproariously and taunted, "Benny, a *preacher*? You'll *never* be a preacher."

My youngest brother, Michael, didn't understand all the commotion. He was only three years old at the time. He was born about one year after we left Israel—the only true Canadian in the family.

"YOU'LL DO WHAT I SAY!"

What a tremendous change came to my life. Early in the morning my big Bible was open and I was drinking in the Word. My major interest that final semester of high school was no longer history, theater, or French. I just wanted to be in those prayer meetings and spend time with my growing circle of born-again friends. And I wasn't shy about sharing my testimony at the kiosk in Fairview Mall.

At night, I'd try any excuse to get out of the house, so I could rush to a youth fellowship or a prayer meeting. Every Thursday night possible, I'd be back at the Catacombs.

The tension I felt in the presence of my father was almost indescribable. When he discovered how often I'd been going to church services, he shouted, "Why do you want to do that? Why?" My father actually believed I was losing my mind.

Dad went to one of his friends and arranged for the man to hire me to work in his factory. In his opinion, I had no choice in the matter. "Benny," my father sternly told me, "you are my son, living in my house, and you will do what I say."

Actually, the idea was, "Let's work him such long hours he won't have time to attend church."

My father drove me to the factory and waited while I went in for the interview. I knew in a split second, however, this was not for me. The boss was one of the toughest, most mean-spirited men I had ever met. I thought, *There's no way I could ever work for this man.*

"Well, when do you start?" my father wanted to know when I got back to the car.

"Father," I replied, "I could never have him for a boss. I'm not working there. I'm going to keep my job at the kiosk."

To be honest, I felt sorry for my dad that day. He was exasperated with me. "Son," he said, "what do you want me to do for you? Tell me what it is. I'll do anything you ask if you'll just please leave this Jesus of yours."

I turned to my father and replied, "You can do anything you want, but I would rather die than give up what I've found."

Almost instantly the atmosphere turned ugly. There was another outburst of ridicule and scorn.

HE WAS SHOCKED!

As the months passed, there was less and less communication with my dad. At the dinner table, I was totally ignored. He acted as if I were not present.

Slowly, my mother's attitude softened. She did her best to be a peacemaker, yet I knew the topic of religion was taboo. Mom earned a few extra dollars by doing alterations and often gave me spending money.

Getting to a prayer meeting, or to a youth service, became an increasing problem. One of the only times my father spoke to me was to say, "Absolutely not" when I asked permission to attend church. In our culture, it was unthinkable to disobey your parents.

As a son still living under the roof of my parents, I did everything in my power to be obedient. Out of respect, I would ask, "Can I go to the meeting tonight?"

"No," he would grumble. And I'd go up to my room to pray, "Please, Lord. Change his mind." Then I'd come back down and ask again.

Once, he warned me, "You can go to that church of yours, but if you mention the name of Jesus just one more time, you'll wish you hadn't!" He threatened to kick me out of the house.

Several weeks later, at home, on a day I was basking in what the Lord was doing in my life, I said without thinking, "Oh, thank You, Jesus."

My father walked over to me and slapped my face. "Remember what I told you?" he growled.

The pain I felt was not because of his slap. I was hurting for the family I loved so much—a family I prayed would one day know and love Jesus as I did.

Over time, knowing I would not give up, my father softened a little.

SEE A PSYCHIATRIST?

Spiritually, I was feasting at a banqueting table.

The Catacombs always brought in outstanding speakers and special guests—who sometimes would never reach the pulpit because of the spirit of praise and worship that descended like a mighty cloud. There were nights the band began playing in the Spirit—cello, violas, trumpets, drums, and a five-rank pipe organ—some of the most beautiful sounds you've ever heard.

You never knew what to expect in those services. One night a group from "The Church of Satan" showed up to raise havoc, only to have three of them come crying to the altar for salvation!

Kids were kicking the drug habit. Thousands of lives were being revolutionized.

On Sundays I began to attend a church pastored by Maxwell Whyte, an outstanding teacher of God's Word who became a spiritual mentor to me. Pastor Whyte was the minister who baptized me in water.

At home, my brothers continued to make fun of me. They would mock charismatic Christians, and laugh at the thought of my someday becoming a preacher. The longer it continued, the more I prayed, "Lord, will it ever end? Will they ever come to know You?"

Somehow, my dad found out that I had been telling my little sister, Mary, about the Lord. Exploding with anger, he yelled, "Don't you ever talk to her again about these things."

About the only member of my family I could talk to was little Michael.

To my parents, the situation was desperate. My father's mother came to visit from Jaffa and tried to convince me to renounce my newfound faith. "Benny, you are an embarrassment to the family name," she said. "Don't you understand the shame you're causing?"

In desperation, my father even made an appointment for me to see a psychiatrist. And what was the doctor's conclusion?

"Perhaps your son is going through a difficult phase. He'll snap out of it."

Looking back, the wall that separated me from my parents must have been in God's divine plan. It caused me to spend hundreds of hours in my room—alone with God. I prayed, I worshiped and studied the Word. There was a strong foundation being established in my life—one I would surely need in the days ahead.

In late 1973, Merv and Merla Watson took me aside and said, "Benny, we have been watching your life and believe God wants to use you. We'd like you to become a member of our praise and worship team at the Catacombs."

Tears welled up in my eyes as I said, "Of course, I'll do it!" Even though I didn't have the ability to speak in public, I knew that God had called me to the ministry—and this was the start.

The next Thursday night I was on the platform at St. Paul's.

My hands were raised to heaven as our team helped lead that huge audience in praises to the Lord. And I remember the night I felt the Spirit move me to speak a psalm, letting the Lord give me the words in the Spirit. Even though my speech was halting and I didn't have command of the language, I knew God was using me.

"SURE, I'LL GO"

"Oh, it was so good to see you on the platform last week," said Jim Poynter, a Free Methodist minister who stopped to buy some ice cream at the Fairview Mall. I had known Jim for several months.

As we talked about the things of the Lord, Jim began telling me about a charter bus trip he was helping arrange to attend one of Kathryn Kuhlman's meetings in Pittsburgh.

I probably didn't show much excitement that day because I had seen her briefly on television and couldn't really relate. I thought she talked rather funny and even looked a little strange. But since Jim was my friend, I said, "That sounds like a good trip. Sure, I'll go with you."

On Thursday, about a week before Christmas in 1973, a packed bus left Toronto about mid-morning. "Jim, you'll never know what a tough time I had with my father about this journey." After a great deal of protest, he grudgingly gave his permission. Other than a Boy Scout camp-out in Israel, I could not remember spending a night away from my family up to this point in my entire life.

Jim Poynter, a gentle-spirited man, was one of the finest Christians I have ever known. Over the years, he and his wife,

Marian, took in more than sixty people off the streets and helped turn their lives around. Many have gone on to be ministers, Christian business leaders, even a university president. Seated near me on the charter bus to Pittsburgh was Alex Parachin, a former drug addict the Poynters reached out to help. He later became the president of a Christian broadcasting outreach in Canada.

The trip to Pittsburgh should have taken seven hours, but we were slowed by a sudden snowstorm. We didn't arrive at our hotel until one o'clock in the morning.

"Benny, we have to be up at five," Jim told me.

"Five in the morning?" I exclaimed. "Why so early?"

"If we are not standing outside the doors of the building by six o'clock, we'll never get a seat," said Jim.

The next morning I had quite a surprise.

CHAPTER 7

"HE'S ALL I'VE GOT"

The scene was difficult to imagine. In the predawn darkness on the streets of downtown Pittsburgh, hundreds of people were standing in the freezing, bitter cold. They filled the sidewalk and steps leading to the First Presbyterian Church—and the doors wouldn't be opening for another two hours!

When Jim Poynter awakened me just one hour earlier, I put on every piece of warm clothing I could find—including snow boots, a wool sweater, heavy coat, and leather gloves.

Since I was smaller in stature than Jim, I began moving closer to the doors—making sure he was right behind me. As the first rays of sunlight began to brighten the scene, I must have looked surprised when I saw people sleeping on the steps. A woman standing next to me commented, "They've been here all night. It's like this every time!"

Suddenly, as I stood there, I felt a most unusual sensation. My body began to vibrate—much as if someone had taken me by the shoulders and begun to shake me. For a second I thought the bitter weather was playing tricks on me. Yet I had plenty of warm clothing on and didn't feel exceptionally cold.

The shaking that came over me was uncontrollable and would not stop. The trembling felt like nothing I had ever experienced. I didn't want to tell Jim, but my very bones were rattling. I could feel it in my legs, my head, and all through my body. I wondered, *What in the world is going on? Could this be the power of God?*

While this continued, the doors of the sanctuary were about to be unlocked and the growing throng of people surged. I was worried that those who were now pressed against me could also feel the vibration.

Jim gave me some last-minute advice. "Benny," he said, "when those doors open, run just as fast as you can."

I asked, "Why?"

He had been to these meetings before and cautioned me, "If you don't hurry, they'll run right over you."

I heeded his advice, and when the doors to First Presbyterian were opened, I ran past everyone in sight—ushers, old people, young people—and quickly reached the front of the sanctuary.

When I attempted to sit down, however, an usher announced, "You can't sit there. That row's reserved." Later I found out that Miss Kuhlman's staff carefully selected the people who would sit in the front row. She was extremely sensitive to the Spirit and wanted only prayed-up positive supporters of her ministry right in front of her.

Unfortunately, the second row was already packed; still, Jim and I were able to claim a good seat on row three.

STILL SHAKING

The service wouldn't be starting for another hour, so I removed my heavy coat, boots, and gloves and relaxed. I realized that the shaking that had begun outside was still there—even more pronounced than before. Now I could feel the pounding throbs and vibrations up and down my arms and legs. It felt as if they were attached to a machine of some kind. This was an experience so unusual to me that I became frightened.

The organist began playing, yet I paid little attention. All my thoughts were focused on this trembling that was affecting me from head to toe. No, I didn't feel sick, or as if I were coming down with a virus. It was just the opposite—and the longer it continued, the more beautiful and peaceful it became. All fear and anxiety left me.

I looked up, and without any announcement, Kathryn Kuhlman appeared. Almost instantly, the atmosphere in that room became electric.

To be honest, I had no idea what to expect. I didn't hear voices, or heavenly angels singing—I only knew my body had been shaking for three solid hours.

A GENTLE BREEZE

Miss Kuhlman led the audience in singing "How Great Thou Art." Spontaneously, I stood to my feet, lifted my hands as high as they would go, and began singing at the top of my lungs:

> Then sings my soul, My Savior, God, to Thee:
> How great Thou art! How great Thou art!

My cheeks became moist—never before had tears welled in my eyes so quickly. I felt lifted into the very presence of God.

I wasn't singing the way I normally sang in church. I sang with my entire being. And when we came to the words, "Then sings my soul," it literally echoed from my soul.

I became so lost in praise that I hardly realized that my shaking had subsided—it had completely stopped.

In the next few minutes of that meeting I thought I had left this planet—raptured into the courts of heaven. The worship was far beyond anything I had experienced in Toronto. I can only describe it as coming face-to-face with pure, spiritual truth. I had no idea what others were feeling. I only knew I was meeting God Himself.

As the glorious worship continued, I felt a gentle breeze begin to blow. And, with my hands still raised, worshiping the Lord, I briefly opened my eyes to see where this draft of wind was coming from. It was like a soft breeze—very gentle, very slow.

I lifted my head back and looked up at the stained-glass windows. They weren't open, and, besides, they were much too high to allow in such a draft.

What was this unusual breeze? In many ways it felt like a current of air—moving down one of my arms and up the other.

I wondered, *What is happening? Could I ever dare tell anyone what I feel? They would never understand this.*

The waves of that wind continued to wash over me for what seemed like ten minutes. Next, I felt as if my body were being wrapped in a warm, pure blanket.

"HAVE MERCY"

On the platform, Miss Kuhlman began ministering to the people, though I hardly noticed. I was totally lost in the Spirit—feeling the Lord closer to me than ever in my existence.

At that moment I felt an overwhelming urge to talk to the Lord, yet all I could quietly say was, "Dear Jesus, please have mercy on me." I repeated those words again, "Jesus, please have mercy on me."

I felt so unworthy to be receiving such an outpouring of God's love. I was much like Isaiah when he entered the presence of the Lord. He cried, "Woe is me, for I am undone! Because I am a man of unclean lips, and I dwell in the midst of a people of unclean lips; for my eyes have seen the King, the LORD of hosts" (Isa. 6:5).

A similar thing occurred when people met Jesus. They saw their own filth—and their desperate need to be cleansed. In that beautiful sanctuary, with a noted woman evangelist speaking from the platform, that is exactly what was happening to Benny Hinn. The searchlight of heaven illumined my heart. I could clearly see my faults, my imperfections, my weaknesses, and my sins.

Over and over I pleaded, "Dear Jesus, please have mercy on me."

Suddenly I heard the unmistakable voice of the Lord. Gently, He said to me, "My mercy is abundant on you."

Since the day I became a Christian, I had prayed to the Lord. And now He was talking to me! I wanted this communion to last forever.

As the service progressed, I continued to quietly cry without shame or embarrassment. What life had to offer could never compare with this. I was being transformed by the Spirit and nothing else was important. This was what the Word describes as "peace . . . which surpasses all understanding" (Phil. 4:7).

In the midst of this glorious worship, the words of the Lord kept ringing in my ears: "My mercy is abundant on you."

WHY IS SHE CRYING?

I had heard from Jim Poynter and others about the incredible miracles that had taken place in Miss Kuhlman's services, yet I wasn't prepared for what I was about to witness. For the next three hours people streamed to the front of the auditorium, anxious to give testimony to the healings that were taking place—in that very meeting.

I watched a woman rise from her wheelchair. People who were deaf suddenly could hear. There were others healed of arthritis, headaches, tumors, and other infirmities.

Oh, what a service that was! I had never been so moved and touched by God's power.

As the meeting continued and I was quietly praying, I realized that everything had become hushed. I immediately thought, *Please, Lord, don't ever let this meeting end.*

When I looked up, Miss Kuhlman's head was buried in her hands—and she began to sob. As her sobs became louder and louder, every person in the room halted their movement. The ushers didn't move a muscle. Every eye was fixed on her.

I wondered, *What could she be crying about?* I had never seen a minister with that kind of reaction—and I was told later that Kathryn had never done anything like this before.

Her sobbing continued for what must have been two minutes. Then, in a flash, her head was thrust back and her eyes were aflame—she was just a few feet in front of me.

Her demeanor instantly changed and she took on a certainty—a holy boldness.

With great emotion and power she pointed her finger out toward the audience. At the same time you could see the lines of pain etched on her countenance.

Filled with obvious agony, and still sobbing, she looked out at the vast throng and said, "Please"— stretching out the word— "Pleeeease, don't grieve the Holy Spirit."

She was literally pleading. "Please," she begged, "don't grieve the Holy Spirit."

Her eyes seemed to be looking straight at me.

As she spoke those words I was motionless, almost afraid to breathe. I had both of my hands on the pew in front of me, wondering, *What will happen next?*

Then Miss Kuhlman said, "Don't you understand? He's all I've got!"

I didn't quite grasp what she meant, yet she continued to plead. "Please! Don't wound Him. He's all I've got. Don't wound the One I love!"

If I live to be 120 I will never forget those words—and how deeply she pleaded.

"MY CLOSEST FRIEND"

Since becoming a born-again believer I had heard many evangelists, ministers, and teachers talk about the Holy Spirit—but not like this. Their teaching had to do with the gifts of the Spirit, tongues, or prophecy—never, "He's my closest, most personal, most intimate, most beloved friend."

What was Kathryn Kuhlman saying? She spoke of a person who was real, who was alive. Next, with great emphasis, she pointed her long finger down at the crowd and said with great confidence, "He's more real to me than you—more real than anything in this world!"

At that moment—when she spoke those words—something penetrated deep inside me. Again I cried and said, "Lord, please let me know You like this."

Since this was my first experience in such a meeting, I thought everyone present would feel what I felt. Now I know that God deals with us as individuals—and I am convinced that much of what took place in that service was prepared by God for me.

Did I fully understand everything that happened in that service? It was not possible. Yet I had no doubt that God's power and reality had transformed my life.

As the service was about to conclude, I looked up and saw what seemed to be a mist that was around and over the head of the woman evangelist. I thought for a moment I had been crying so much it was just me—or an illusion. I looked again and it was real. Through the mist, her face was shining like a light.

Thinking back on that incredible day, I don't feel the Lord was trying to give any glory to Miss Kuhlman. I am convinced, however, that He used that meeting to manifest His awesome power to me.

The people began to file out, yet I didn't want to vacate that pew. Instead, I sat down to reflect on what had just transpired. I thought, *Oh, if my family could only experience what I have just felt.*

I could have lingered there all day, but the bus was waiting. At the back of the sanctuary I paused, turning around one last time. I pondered, "What did she mean? What was she really saying when she talked about her friend, the Holy Spirit?"

All the way back to Toronto I kept thinking, *How could the Holy Spirit be so real to her? Is He really a* person? I asked several people to help me understand, yet they couldn't.

I arrived home totally exhausted—having only four hours of sleep in two days.

But God was not finished with me yet.

CHAPTER 8

"CAN I MEET YOU"

Every bone in my body was aching for sleep, yet my eyes were wide open—my spirit still soaring from this most incredible day.

Then, as I lay stretched out on my bed in Toronto, it seemed that something was tugging at me. I was being pulled off the mattress and onto my knees. The sensation was strange, but I did not resist.

In that dark room, I knew God was at work and I was more than ready to follow His leading.

My heart was filled with questions, and I didn't quite know where to begin. I wondered, *How can I have what that evangelist in Pittsburgh had experienced?* That's what I desired more than anything in this world—to experience the reality of what Kathryn Kuhlman had talked about!

From the moment she uttered the words, "He's more real than anything in this world," I developed a hunger, a craving to know the Holy Spirit in that same dimension. Yet I hardly knew where to begin.

That night on my knees, three days before Christmas, 1973, I knew in my heart what I wanted to say, but how could I express it?

IT'S HAPPENING AGAIN

Since childhood I had heard about the Holy Spirit. He was part of the Trinity, and a member of the Godhead to be worshiped. Never had I thought of Him as a person to be addressed. What words should I use? Where should I start?

I decided to begin the only way I knew—with my own simple vocabulary.

In my bedroom on Crossbow Crescent Street that night, I prayed, "Holy Spirit—Kathryn Kuhlman says You are her friend." I continued, "I don't think I know You. Now, before today I thought I did. But after that meeting I realize I really don't."

In childlike faith I asked, "Can I meet You? Can I really meet You?"

I was greatly concerned about my words. I thought, *Is what I'm saying right? Should I be speaking to the Holy Spirit this way?* Then it occurred to me, *If I am truthful and honest, God will show me whether I'm right or wrong.*

After my feeble attempt to speak to the Holy Spirit, I waited—and waited. There seemed to be no response. Anxious, I began to wonder, *Is there really such an experience as meeting the Holy Spirit? Can it truly happen?*

Then, kneeling on the floor, with my eyes still closed, I felt something that resembled a jolt of electricity. Instantly, my body began to vibrate—almost an exact repeat of the two hours I waited in the cold outside the church in Pittsburgh—and what I felt for another hour in the sanctuary.

Oh. It's happening again, I thought. This time, however, I was in my own warm room, dressed in my pajamas. Still the trembling was the same.

I didn't want to open my eyes. It seemed everything that happened to me in the service was now taking place at once. Yes, I was shaking, but I also felt the warm, soft blanket of God's presence draped around me. How could heaven be any greater?

There He was—the Holy Spirit had entered my room. And He was as real as the bed I was kneeling beside. For the next several hours I was crying and laughing at the same time. It was as though my bedroom had been lifted into heaven itself. Nothing in my twenty-one years could compare with this visitation. It was joy unspeakable!

If my mother and father—who were just down the hall—had known what their son was experiencing, I'm sure they would have exploded. How could they ever understand?

TALKING WITH MY FRIEND

From the moment the Holy Spirit made Himself real that night, He was no longer a nebulous concept, or a far-off invisible "third person" of the Trinity. He was alive—He had a personality.

When I finally opened my eyes, I was surprised to find that I was still in my room, kneeling on the same floor—the power of God's Spirit still tingling in my body.

In the early hours of the morning, I dropped off to sleep, unaware of the miracle that God had wrought in me.

The sun was barely rising on that crisp Canadian morning—but I was wide awake. I was anxious to talk once more to my newfound friend.

The first words out of my mouth were, "Good morning, Holy Spirit!"

The instant I uttered them, that same heavenly atmosphere permeated the room. The shaking and vibrating were gone; I felt the warmth and peace of His presence.

Those words seemed so natural for me to say. "Good morning, Holy Spirit." I was conversing with my friend—the same friend that Kathryn Kuhlman had talked about.

I have been asked, "Is that the night you were filled with the Spirit?"

That experience in my bedroom was far beyond speaking in tongues. Oh yes, I spoke in a heavenly language, yet what I am sharing with you is far beyond tongues. I was filled with His *presence*. For the first time, I met the person of the Holy Spirit. And from that moment forward He became my counselor, my companion, my friend.

NOT BY MIGHT

After welcoming the Spirit that remarkable day, I opened my Bible, not knowing where to begin. As I turned back the cover of the Holy Book, I felt Him there—as if He were sitting right beside me. My eyes did not see His face or gaze upon His countenance, but I was keenly aware of where He was in my room. And, starting with that day, I began to know His personality.

For nearly two years, since I gave my life to Christ, I had diligently studied God's Word. Now, the Bible took on incredible substance and a totally new dimension. When I had a question, I would say, "Holy Spirit, show it to me in the Word." And He did!

For example, He directed me to John 16:14: "He will glorify Me, for He will take of what is Mine, and declare it to you."

And I understood that He came to glorify and magnify Jesus.

I learned that only the Holy Spirit can reveal Jesus to the hearts of men. "But when the Helper comes, whom I shall send to you from the Father, the Spirit of truth who proceeds from the Father, He will testify of Me" (John 15:26).

I wanted to know why He had come, and He pointed me to these words: "We have received, not the spirit of the world, but the Spirit who is from God, that we might know the things that have been freely given to us by God" (1 Cor. 2:12).

To say that the Bible became alive is an understatement. I now understood the authority of the words: "'Not by might nor by power, but by My Spirit,' says the LORD" (Zech. 4:6).

Through Scripture, He affirmed the awesome transformation that was taking place in my life. Morning after morning, day after day, I grew to know my friend.

To me, the most dramatic change occurred in my prayer life. I said, "Holy Spirit, since You know the Father so well, would You help me pray?"

With the Spirit's guidance, I began to call on the Father. It was as if I had had a personal introduction to the Almighty.

I remember I had questions concerning the fatherhood of God. The Spirit opened the Word and pointed to this passage: "As many as are led by the Spirit of God, these are sons of God. For you did not receive the spirit of bondage again to fear, but you received the Spirit of adoption by whom we cry out, 'Abba, Father'" (Rom. 8:14–15).

I thought about what Jesus said concerning the Holy Spirit— that He would be our comforter, teacher, and guide. Now this heavenly instructor had become my friend.

For the first time I understood what Jesus meant when He

told His disciples to follow Him—and then later told them the Holy Spirit would guide them into all truth. I began to understand that only the Spirit of God can cause us to follow the Lord.

In my room, I was receiving an education greater than any university or seminary could offer. My teacher was the Spirit Himself.

For days, weeks, then months, my search of the Scriptures continued and my questions were being answered. Even more, I felt His strength and might. There were times I would literally have to prop myself up against the bed because of the intensity and the power of the Holy Spirit I felt in my room. At other moments He was gentle and tender—and the love I felt was greater than anything I had ever known.

THE TRAIN

My parents immediately recognized that something unusual had taken place. If you think they were upset at my conversion, you should have seen them now! Whether it was confusion, consternation, or conviction I wasn't sure, nevertheless I felt their growing wrath.

Outside my home, the reaction was totally reversed. Several of my Christian friends were already buzzing about the fact that there had been a major transformation in my life. "Something has definitely happened to Benny," they would tell their friends.

About one week after my encounter, Jim Poynter picked me up and drove me to the apartment of Alex Parachin and his wife. Alex had been with us on the excursion to Pittsburgh.

I had been talking by phone with Jim about some of the

miraculous things that had transpired in the past few days—
including a vision God had allowed me to see.

"Tell Alex what happened," Jim insisted. "Tell him about your
vision."

Looking at me, I'm sure the Parachins wondered, *How could
the Lord ever use somebody like Benny?* My long hair was sticking
out under a beanie cap that was pulled down tight over my ears.
They also knew I could hardly complete a sentence without
stammering.

That afternoon, in their dining room, I shared with them a
most unusual vision. "I was traveling on a railroad car that had
no walls," I told them. "It was just an open, flatbed car."

I explained that I was seated in the middle of the car that was
being pulled by a powerful locomotive. "Sitting all around me
were a great number of people," I said. "Suddenly, the train
started picking up speed, going faster and faster."

The ride turned to chaos as the train began tearing around
corners. "People began falling off the car," I explained. "Yet I
stayed in the center. And the only reason I didn't suffer the
same fate was because of a power that was coming down on
top of my head. It was safely holding me in place while the
locomotive picked up steam."

As I continued explaining the vision, the Holy Spirit filled
that dining room to such an extent, Alex fell to the floor under
God's power.

Later, Jim talked with me concerning what the Lord had
revealed. From that first week when the Spirit enveloped my life,
Jim felt that I would be involved in a most unique ministry. He
said, "Benny, God is going to launch you into ministry with
incredible speed. And there will be many people who will try to

go along for the ride, but they will fall by the wayside. God is telling me that if you remain close to Him, you will stay centered—exactly where He wants you to be."

IT COULD NOT BE CONTAINED

A few days later, Jim Poynter asked if I would go with him to a service he was asked to conduct for Rev. Weldon Johnson—who was starting a new church in a school. It was announced as a healing service.

Many of those in the congregation were people who had gone to Pittsburgh on one of the charter buses Jim had helped to arrange. A large number of them were Latvians.

That night, Jim led the singing with his accordion. After a word of testimony, he called those forward who wanted a special touch from God. He also asked me to join him at the altar to help him lay hands on the people.

Hallelujah! God was faithful. The Spirit that had anointed me in my room overflowed to those close by.

I thank God for those Latvian people. They not only felt God's power, they began to pray for me as if I were one of their sons. Even before I had ever preached, they were some of my early prayer warriors.

I remember the afternoon Jim and his wife invited me to attend a Methodist church where they were conducting a meeting. Having spent the entire day searching the Word and delighting in the anointing of the Spirit, I thought this would be a perfect ending for my day. I was anxious to go.

When I heard Jim honking the car horn, I ran down the stairs, still feeling the Lord's presence on me.

The moment I jumped into the front seat and shut the door, Jim began to weep, and started to sing the chorus, "Alleluia! Alleluia!" He turned to me and said, "Benny, can you feel the Holy Spirit's presence in this car?"

"Yes, I can," I responded.

Jim could hardly drive. He continued to weep before the Lord.

ABSOLUTELY AMAZED

"Would you mind if I went along?" I asked Alex Parachin, when he told me he was going to give his testimony of how he was delivered from drugs.

The service was at Faith Temple, a church pastored by Winston I. Nunes, one of the most remarkable Spirit-led ministers who ever lived. At the conclusion of the meeting, Dr. Nunes stood and announced, "I feel God wants these young men to minister around the altar tonight, not me."

Even though I had not participated in the service, Alex motioned for me to come forward. As I began laying my hands on people, the power of God began falling. I was startled— absolutely amazed at what God was doing.

Meanwhile, I continued to go with Jim Poynter to hold healing services for Weldon Johnson—where the Latvians attended. The crowds not only were growing, but one night we drove up to see a long line of people queuing outside the door, waiting to get in. I was astonished.

"What's going on?" I asked Jim.

"May I tell you something," Jim quietly responded. "Word is getting around that there is a young man by the name of Benny who has the anointing of the Holy Spirit on his life. These dear people just want to be near that anointing."

Those precious Latvians were the early supporters of my "ministry"—a ministry that had not really begun.

That night again, after Jim spoke, there was a powerful presence of the Lord. We prayed for people and many were blessed greatly by the power of God.

The train was beginning to move—and it was picking up speed.

CHAPTER 9

Would I Be Left Behind

As I look back at what the Lord has done, even selling ice cream was part of God's divine plan that led me to where I am at this moment. You see, it was in that little shop where I met Jim Poynter, who told me about a woman evangelist by the name of Kathryn Kuhlman. I traveled with him to a service in Pittsburgh, Pennsylvania, that dramatically transformed my entire future.

After my job at the Fairview Mall, I accepted a position as a filing clerk for the Catholic School Board in Toronto, where the Lord continued His intense work in my heart.

When I left the house in the morning, the Holy Spirit would go with me. At times I actually felt Someone beside me. On the way to work, traveling on the bus, I would often feel the urge to start conversing with Him. And I would begin to pray for the salvation of those on the bus—the Holy Spirit burdened me for their souls.

The minute my workday was over, I rushed home to continue my fellowship with the Lord. My room became a sacred haven, and when I was not working, I would often stay home just to commune with Him.

"What I want is what I have right now," I told the Lord during those days. "Whatever it is, don't let it end." I began to understand more fully the apostle Paul's desire for "the fellow-ship of the Holy Spirit."

A ROARING INFERNO

One day in April 1974, I asked the Lord, "Why are You bless-ing me in this way?" and "Why are all these things happening to me?" For I knew that God surely did not impart His presence for spiritual picnics.

Then suddenly, with my eyes wide open as I began to pray, I saw someone standing in front of me. That person was totally engulfed in flames and I could not tell whether it was a man or a woman. His or her feet were not touching the ground. The mouth of this being was opening and closing—similar to what the Word describes as "gnashing of teeth."

As I saw this person enveloped in tormenting flames, I cried, "No! No! No!"—not knowing why I said that.

In that moment the Lord spoke to me in an audible voice. He said, "Preach the gospel."

My response was, "But Lord, I can't talk."

Later that night the Lord gave me a dream in which I saw an angel. He carried a chain in his hand, attached to a door that seemed to fill the heavens. He pulled open the door, and there were people as far as the eye could see. Then he took me to a higher place.

Looking at that same crowd, I saw they were all moving toward a large, deep valley that was a roaring inferno of fire. It was terrifying. I saw thousands of people falling into that blaz-ing abyss. Those on the front lines were trying to resist, but the crush of humanity pushed them into the flames.

Again, the Lord spoke very distinctly and said, "If you do not preach, every soul who falls will be your responsibility."

This was the second time the Lord had made it clear that I was to minister His Word—once at the time of my conversion, and now through this vision. I knew that everything occurring in my life was for one purpose only: to proclaim the gospel.

Someone recently asked, "Benny, if you had not met Jesus, what do you think your life would have become?"

When I was seventeen or eighteen, I believed that someday I would go into politics, or perhaps find employment in the travel industry. Thank God, all of that was reordered when Christ made Himself real—and showed me my future.

"DEAR JOURNAL"

During these momentous times I kept daily journals—which are now some of my most treasured possessions. It was not a diary with typical entries such as, "Tonight I went to the Catacombs," or "I'm having a difficult time with my father today." Instead, this was a personal account of my spiritual journey. Day after day I faithfully recorded what I had learned from the Word, and what God was teaching me.

At the beginning of 1974 I wrote:

> Lord, make my life full of You.
> Let every day belong to You.
> Let every moment be with You.
> Let me live for Your glory.
> May my days give You praise
> and may my heart give You love

and adoration. May Jesus be all to me,
every moment of every day.

The Spirit of the Lord was not only on me, He even began to saturate our home—so much so that my brothers and sisters began to develop a spiritual hunger. One by one they came to me and began to ask questions. They'd say, "Benny, I've been watching you. This Jesus is real, isn't He?"

My sister Mary gave her heart to the Lord first, and within the next few months my little brothers Sammy and Willie got saved. All I could do was rejoice! A miracle was taking place in our home—and I had not even begun to preach.

As you can imagine, my father was outraged. Was he losing his whole family to this Jesus? He didn't know how to handle the situation. My parents had already seen the turnaround in me—and now were witnessing the same phenomenon in more of their children.

"HIGH PRAISES"

Whenever there was a charter bus going to a Kathryn Kuhlman meeting in Pittsburgh, I did my best to be on board. I was captivated by her ministry—and listened to her almost every night from the powerful 50,000-watt radio station WWVA in Wheeling, West Virginia.

I was not only being fed by the Spirit Himself, but by a host of God's chosen servants. In addition to the Thursday night meetings at the Catacombs, you could often find me at a place called Bezek—a Friday night charismatic meeting in Campbellville, about thirty miles southwest of Toronto.

The services were held in a retreat center that was the vision of Bernie Warren, a United Church of Canada pastor who launched the ministry after receiving the baptism of the Holy Spirit. He named the center Bezek after the place where the Israelites gathered to be refreshed and encouraged as they faced an important battle (1 Sam. 11).

During the week it was an oasis for the counseling of alcoholics, those wanting to get off drugs, and people with other needs. Every Friday night, however, it hosted a charismatic meeting—something rather new to the mainline churches in the area.

There was an unusual freedom of worship in those services. People lifted their hands and would often "sing in tongues." Some nights we were led by the Spirit into "High Praises." As Psalm 149:6 declares, "Let the high praises of God be in their mouth."

Many brought their musical instruments—trumpets, tambourines, drums, guitars, banjos, flutes and violins. Members of a fellowship called the House of Philadelphia joined in with "Davidic worship," called by many, "dancing before the Lord."

In those meetings I was lost in the awesome presence of God, and grew from the Word I received from Bernie Warren.

On June 10, 1974, my journal reads:

After I came from Bezek, I had a wonderful experience in my room. As I was praying, my heart was filled with joy—and peace was all over my room. Oh, it was so beautiful. I was praying at about one-thirty or two o'clock (and) suddenly, I felt a hand touch me. It was soft and landed on my heart. My heart suddenly started beating and the hand stayed for about thirty seconds. As I felt the hand, a tremendous warm feeling came over me. My whole body was over-whelmed with that tremendous feeling of heat. I knew the Lord touched me. Jesus came and touched me. Oh, His love. It is higher than all heavens. Oh, the deep, deep love of Jesus.

PACKING MY BAGS

Beginning with a summer workshop in 1973, Merv and Merla Watson organized what they called "Shekinah"—a major production of worship and praise unlike anything that had ever been presented. And they asked me to be part of the team.

The music was first-class, with singers, inspirational dancers, and banners. We were not just going through the motions, this was a dramatic presentation with great anthems such as "Prepare Ye the Way of the Lord," and "Awake, O Israel."

Most of the music was written and arranged by the Watsons, who were classically trained. More than ninety young people participated in the first concert in Toronto.

So great was the response that the decision was made to take the production to Europe for a two-and-a-half-month tour in the summer of 1974. Oh, how I longed to be part of that experience.

Starting early that spring, Monday night rehearsals were scheduled in preparation for the announced tour. As summer grew near, sixty-three people were planning to go to Europe—including me.

There were only two small problems. First, my father absolutely forbade me to go. Second, I had no funds for such a trip—and no idea of how to obtain any.

In prayer, however, my faith came alive and I was convinced that God would make a way. In fact, I was so confident that I began to make preparations, and packed my bags. Still, I had no money and no ticket! The Monday night before the team was to depart for England, I was there for the final rehearsal. "Lord," I prayed, "didn't You tell me I would be spending this summer with 'Shekinah'?"

Was I wrong? Would I be left behind?

CHAPTER 10

SHEKINAH

"How are You going to do it, Lord?" I prayed as the final Monday night "Shekinah" rehearsal began. I knew that I was going to Europe as much as I knew my name.

About halfway through the session, Merv Watson took me aside and said, "Benny, Merla and I have been praying, and the Lord told us to provide your plane fare"—and he handed me the Air Canada ticket.

"Oh, this is wonderful," I exclaimed. "This is marvelous!"

I was absolutely overwhelmed by their generosity. Later, I learned that the Watsons had mortgaged their home to make the summer journey possible.

The moment the rehearsal was over, I rushed home to tell my parents that I was leaving that week for Europe. "See, here is the ticket!" I said, opening the envelope.

"Who gave you that?" replied my father angrily. "Did you bribe someone?"

"No," I told him. "It was a gift, from some people who really want me to be on this trip."

"Fine," he gruffed. "Just go, then." And he reached into his pocket and handed me $25. To me, that gesture was amazing— it was as if he had handed me $25,000.

On June 18, 1974, just as I was leaving for the airport, my

father said, "When you get there, call collect and ask for yourself." That way he would know I had arrived and wouldn't have
to pay for the call.

"I can't do that, Dad," I responded. "It would be lying. Don't
worry, I'm still going to call you."

"You'd better not call me without making it collect," he continued to insist.

The next day I went to the Toronto airport with my ticket,
my suitcase, and $25.

What an adventure it was!

The first afternoon I arrived at the home of a beautiful family near London who were involved in Youth with a Mission. I
immediately asked, "May I use your phone? I need to call my
parents to let them know I arrived safely." And I added, "I'll
pay you for the call." I was going to give them part of the $25
that was in my pocket

"Certainly. Go right ahead," the man of the house insisted.

I picked up the phone and dialed "0" for operator and a
woman came on the line. "Excuse me, sir," she said. "I know this
may sound like a strange question, but are you a Christian?"

I was in shock, wondering, *Who had I reached? And how did
she know?*

"Yes, I am," I quickly responded. "I am a Christian."

As God is my witness, the operator said, "The Lord let me
know you would be calling and He told me to pay for your call."

At that point I didn't know whether the person I was speaking to was from England, Canada, or heaven!

In her professional voice, she asked, "What number would
you like me to dial, please?"

It was late at night, Toronto time, and my dad answered the

phone. "This is Benny," I told him. "I just wanted you to know that I made it to England. Everything is fine. I'm staying with some very nice people."

"I thought I told you to call me collect!" he snapped.

"Don't worry, I'm not paying for this call," I quickly responded.

After a couple of curse words, he said, "Those poor people in England—you're doing this to them?"

"No, Dad, they're not paying for it either," I replied.

Obviously aggravated, he retorted, "What kind of Christian are you, lying about this?"

"Oh, you wouldn't understand," I told him. And he hung up the phone.

A DOUBLE-DECKER

The word *Shekinah* speaks of God's dwelling place, presence, and glory. That's what we earnestly prayed would happen to every person who attended the nightly concerts—that God's glory would touch their life.

Our transportation was a double-decker bus that a Christian man in England let the Watsons have for just one British pound. Behind the bus were two trucks filled with production equipment and our suitcases.

Most nights we were hosted by individual families and I began to meet the most wonderful Christians.

The concerts, held in gothic cathedrals, concert halls, and large churches, were spectacular. When sixty-three Spirit-filled young people began to worship the Lord through soul-stirring music, dramatic pageant, and dance, the audiences immediately joined in praise. Many of the songs we sang were written by

Merla Watson—including one that became a worldwide favorite: "Jehovah Jireh, My Provider, His Grace Is Sufficient for Me."

We even performed an open-air concert at Trafalgar Square in downtown London.

Almost every morning we had a chapel service, and were blessed by the ministry of outstanding local preachers and Bible teachers.

As I look back at my journal, I realize that it was not the beautiful edifices or tourist attractions that held my attention. My one great desire was to be close to the Savior.

In England, on June 26, 1974, I wrote:

> Dear Jesus. Take this day and make it Yours. Please place in my heart that fire and love for You. Lord Jesus, take my thoughts and make them Yours. May I think on You alone today, Lord. Please help me, Holy Spirit, and use me for Jesus' sake. Amen.

LESSONS OF FAITH

The tour wound its way through Belgium, Germany, and Switzerland. And on Sunday morning, August 18, 1974, in Holland, we had the memorable experience of attending the home church of Corrie ten Boom. Corrie, author of *The Hiding Place,* spoke that morning on the importance of total surrender. Her unforgettable message was titled "The Glove"—and what it means to place our life in the Master's hand.

Corrie illustrated the message with a glove in her hand, telling us that "we are the glove and the hand is the Lord—and as we surrender ourselves, one part at a time, the Lord fits the glove." It was a message I began to put into practice.

After a final concert in Holland, we headed for home on the

fifth of September. I was restless—knowing that God was calling me to be more than just part of a singing group. Financially, God used that journey to teach me what it means to step out in faith.

My money grew and multiplied. With absolutely no prompting, total strangers came up to me and said, "Here, the Lord told me to give you this."

I returned to Toronto with new clothes and new luggage. And I said to my father, "Dad, I want to thank you for the twenty-five dollars," as I handed it back to him.

He just shook his head.

IT HAPPENED AT SHILO

The entire fall of 1974, my fellowship with the Holy Spirit intensified. Yet there was a burden on my heart that grew heavier.

Finally, in November, I couldn't avoid the subject any longer. I said to the Lord, "I will preach the gospel on one condition: that You will be with me in every service." And then I reminded Him, "Lord, You know that I can't talk." I worried continually about my speech problem and the fact that I was going to embarrass myself.

Still embedded in my mind's eye was the picture of the burning man—and the sound of the Lord saying, "If you do not preach, everyone who falls will be your responsibility."

I thought, *I must begin to preach.* But wouldn't passing out tracts be good enough?

One afternoon, the first week of December, I was sitting in the home of Stan and Shirley Phillips in Oshawa, about thirty miles east of Toronto.

"Can I tell you something?" I asked. Never before had I felt led to share with anyone the full story of my experiences, dreams, and visions. For nearly three hours, I poured out my heart, including details only the Lord and I knew. I told them of my increasing heavy burden for lost souls.

Before I had finished, Stanley stopped me and said, "Benny, tonight you must come to our church and share your heart." They had a fellowship called Shilo—about a hundred people at the Trinity Assembly of God in Oshawa. The church was pastored by the Reverend Kenneth Beesley, whose son, Gary, would one day join the ministerial staff of the World Outreach Church in Orlando.

I phoned Marilyn Stroud and asked her to help with the music. I had known her for nearly two years—she was part of the Catacombs praise and worship team and was on the "Shekinah" journey.

I wish you could have seen me. My hair tumbled down to my shoulders, and I hadn't dressed for church because the invitation had been totally unexpected.

That night, December 7, 1974, Stan Phillips introduced me to the group, and for the first time in my life I stood behind a pulpit to preach.

The instant I opened my mouth, I felt something touch my tongue and it was loosened. There were a few seconds of numbness, then I began to proclaim God's Word with absolute fluency.

Here's what was amazing. God didn't heal me when I was sitting in the audience. He didn't heal me when I was walking up to the platform. He didn't heal me when I stood behind the pulpit. God performed the miracle when I opened my mouth.

The moment my tongue loosened, I said to myself, "That's it!" The stuttering was gone, all of it—and it has never returned. Thank You, Jesus!

After my message, I invited people to come forward to be prayed for. About ten responded. No one knew about being slain in the Spirit, yet as I prayed for these dear people, they began falling under God's anointing. When I looked up, almost everyone in the building was coming to the front for prayer. What a mighty work the Lord did that night!

"Benny, when you began to speak, my jaw dropped open," Marilyn Stroud told me after the service. "What I saw tonight was a miracle."

SIX STRAPPING DUTCHMEN

The next day Marilyn phoned Bernie Warren at the Bezek center in Campbellville and asked, "Do you remember Benny Hinn?"

"Of course I do," replied Bernie. He thought of me as "just one of the kids" who came out to the meetings from the Catacombs.

"Well, you need to see him," said Marilyn, "because something special is happening in his life. It would be great if you could have him come and minister to your people."

I went to see Bernie Warren at Bezek the following Friday and shared with him what had happened to me in Oshawa. We talked about the manifestations and people being powerfully touched by the Holy Spirit. Our conversation continued until late in the afternoon. I felt honored that this highly respected minister had spent this time with me.

"Benny, I feel led to ask you to participate in the service tonight," said Bernie. "Expound on what you are telling me."

Of course, I eagerly agreed.

Hundreds of people were packed into the center that evening. After a short message, the Spirit led me to call people forward. The first to respond were six big, strapping Dutchmen; they towered over me.

I prayed and, *boom,* down they went—all of them! The altars were quickly filled and many were blessed and healed that night by the power of God.

At the close of the meeting, Bernie Warren stepped to the microphone and announced, "Ladies and gentlemen, I know some of you may have questions about what you have witnessed here tonight. But I want you to know that I affirm the ministry the Lord has given to Benny Hinn."

"SOMETHING I WAS NOT EXPECTING"

On the last day of 1974, I sat down with my journal and wrote a summary of the marvelous events that had transpired:

Nineteen seventy-four has been the greatest year I've had. And I know that 1975 will even be a greater year, full of service for the Lord Jesus. I just pray that I may love Him more than ever. All of last year . . . I've experienced a tremendous fellowship with the Lord. Jesus was never so close, the Holy Spirit was never so real. Many times in prayer I've experienced His presence, which brought me great joy and love and peace. There were times I could not stand properly because His presence was with me. My love for Jesus grew in a great way and the Holy Spirit has worked to make Jesus the center of my life. I had many hard trials and tests, but it seemed as though each trial brought me closer to Jesus.

As I look back, I am simply amazed at the change that has taken place and the things I've learned that I don't think I'll ever forget. The Holy Spirit has truly done some great things. He has caused me to come to the cross when my sins were before me. He has given me a great desire to serve the Lord and a hunger to be fully His. He has caused death to come upon the areas of self, and still more He will crucify. He has placed a burden for souls and a love I've never known. Truly I've changed from Glory to Glory.

I came home (from the Shekinah trip to Europe) hungry and thirsty for His closeness and fellowship, and for almost two months all I did was pray and pour my heart out. These were very hard months for me because the Holy Spirit was doing deep work that hurts. But how thankful I am, for He made me a better man, having more of Jesus and His love.

For these two months I had a great hunger and longing to serve the Lord, so I started to pray that God would show me His will, and so He did by placing in my heart this burden for souls. I always knew I would one day preach the gospel, but now it was stronger than ever. I knew I had to do something, but didn't know what or how. At the same time the Holy Spirit was preparing something I was not expecting.

In my journal I wrote the account of Stan and Shirley Phillips inviting me to give my testimony at their church in Oshawa— and the wonderful power of God that descended. And here are the final words I wrote on the last day of 1974:

This started this ministry, which is the ministry of the Holy Spirit . . . and the Lord is moving in a mighty way. I know that I have nothing to do with anything that happens and I pray to God I never will, for my longing is only to preach the gospel and to see souls saved. Jesus, use me only for Your glory. For Your sake, Amen.

That Christmas I had much to celebrate. At the age of twenty-two I had preached my first sermon and had seen God confirm His Word with signs following. And the impediment that had plagued me since childhood was completely healed.

Praise God, my stuttering was gone!

He touched me! Oh, He touched me!

CHAPTER 11

TWO O'CLOCK
IN THE MORNING

"Benny, we believe God wants to use you in a mighty way," my friend Jim Poynter told me—speaking for a group of ministers who had asked me to conduct some meetings in Willowdale, a suburb of Toronto. "We're going to rent the cafeteria of a public school and leave the rest up to the Lord."

It was February 1975, just two months after I had first shared my testimony at the church in Oshawa.

This confirmed the unmistakable voice of the Holy Spirit prompting me that it was time to begin conducting weekly meetings in Toronto. The Lord said, "Follow Me. Hear My voice, and many will be led to Christ."

The ministers in Willowdale were taking quite a chance. I certainly had no track record as an evangelist. I was simply a young man who had turned his life completely over to the Lord. Those who gathered in the cafeteria that night did not know what to expect, and neither did I!

Because of Poynter's connections as a Free Methodist, people from that denomination came out in force. In fact, some of their ministers wanted me to become ordained by that church.

At Willowdale we conducted several services before I felt led to ask those who needed a healing touch from God to come forward for prayer. In those days I formed a "healing line" and personally prayed for those individuals who requested prayer. The Lord began to do some marvelous things. People were delivered from serious addictions, families were reunited, and there were testimonies of miracles. The emphasis, however, was on salvation, and each service always included an invitation for people to find Christ.

During these early days of ministry I was extremely naive. And as the crowds grew, there were all kinds of people desiring to be part of the services. For example, if someone told me, "The Lord has given me a song for the meeting tonight," I would let them sing. Or, if someone had "a word from God," I'd let them share.

It wasn't long, however, until I realized some were hearing their own voice and I asked the Lord to give me discernment.

Despite my immaturity, the crowds grew.

"I think we need to find a larger auditorium and continue these services," said one of the sponsoring ministers. To my delight, we moved to Georges Vanier Secondary School where I had once attended—the same building where I had asked the Lord to come into my heart at a student-led early morning prayer meeting.

Many people from ethnic backgrounds attended those Monday night services in 1975, especially the Latvians.

I am the first to admit that my early sermons had little content. They were basically my testimony of the work of the Spirit—of how He made Himself real to me. In those days I really didn't know too much about organizing my thoughts and preparing a message. I simply communicated from the depths of my heart.

The ministry began to mushroom. It seemed that nearly

every day I was invited to a church or fellowship group to minister. The services were totally led by the Spirit, and I listened intently to His voice. I felt in the perfect center of God's will.

"PRAY, JIM, PRAY!"

At home, there was still such tremendous tension I didn't dare tell my parents that I was actually preaching. They had no inkling. Keeping it quiet for so long was a miracle in itself. My brothers and sisters were aware, but they didn't tell Dad because they knew it would be the end of me!

Also, since there was so little communication around the house, my mother and father didn't know I had been healed of my speech impediment. There had always been times when I could speak without a noticeable problem for a short period— before something set the stuttering off again.

In April 1975, a newspaper ad with my picture appeared in the *Toronto Star*. I was preaching at a little pentecostal church on the west side of Toronto, and the pastor wanted to attract some visitors.

It worked. Unknown to me, my parents, Costandi and Clemence, thumbed through the paper and spotted the ad.

That Sunday night, as I was seated on the platform, I looked up during the song service and could hardly believe my eyes. Coming in the door were my mother and father—being ushered to a seat toward the back of the auditorium.

This is it! I thought. *What's going to happen to me?*

I don't think I've been as frightened in my life. My heart almost stopped, and I could feel the perspiration on my forehead.

My worst nightmare could not have matched this. I was petrified—too startled to laugh and too shocked to cry.

Seated next to me on the platform was my faithful friend, Jim Poynter. I leaned over to him and whispered, "Pray, Jim. Pray!"

He was shocked when I told him my mother and dad were there.

Immediately, a thousand thoughts flashed through my mind, not the least of which was, *Lord, I'll know I am really healed if I don't stutter tonight.* During the four previous months there was never a time I was so nervous during a service—and anxiety always made me stutter.

"Lord, You've got to help me," I prayed as I stepped to the pulpit to preach. Then, as I opened my mouth, words began flowing out of me like a river. I found myself actually "listening" to what the Spirit directed me to say.

I must tell you, however, that I could not bring myself to look in the direction of my parents, not even for a fleeting glance.

As I preached, I knew that my concern about stuttering was needless. God had healed me, and the healing was permanent.

When I had finished my message, I could feel the power of God all through that auditorium. I asked those who needed a healing to come forward for prayer. I kept wondering, *What must my mom and dad be thinking of all this?*

As people came to the altar, I noticed my parents slip from their seats and exit the back door.

When the service was over, I slumped down in one of the pulpit chairs and said, "Jim, you've really got to pray. Do you realize that in the next few hours my destiny will be decided?" Dreading the inevitable confrontation, I told him, "I may have to sleep at your house tonight."

LISTENING IN DISBELIEF

I went out to the parking lot and climbed into my two-door Pontiac—the first car I had ever owned. It was white, with a red vinyl roof. I had bought it from my brother Willie.

For the next several hours I drove aimlessly around Toronto, determined to wait until at least two in the morning to go home. I couldn't bear the thought of facing my parents and knew by that time they would probably be sleeping.

Quietly, just after two o'clock in the morning, I parked in front of the house and turned off the ignition. Then I tiptoed up the steps and slowly turned the key in the lock.

When I opened the front door I was startled by what I saw. There in front of me, seated on the couch, were my mom and dad. I had been panic-stricken when I saw them walk into that church, but this was even worse. My knees began to tremble, and I looked for a place to sit down.

My father was the first to speak and I listened in disbelief.

"Son," he said softly, "how can we become like you?"

Was I hearing what I thought I was hearing? Was this the same man who had been so offended by my conversion? The father who had absolutely forbidden the name of Jesus to be spoken in our home?

"We really want to know," he said. "Tell us how we can have what you have."

I looked at my dear mother and saw tears begin to fall down her beautiful cheeks. I couldn't contain my joy at that moment. I began to weep. And for the next hour of that unforgettable night I opened the Scriptures and led my parents to the saving knowledge of the Lord Jesus Christ.

At one point my daddy said, "Benny, do you know what convinced me?" He told me that when I began preaching, he turned to my mother and said, "That's not your son. Your son can't talk! His God must be real."

The marvelous conversion of my parents allowed the Lord to literally sweep through the rest of the family. Mary, Sammy, and Willie had already given their hearts to Christ, and now it happened to Henry, Rose, and my little brother Mike. The last one to come into the fold was Chris. If you've ever heard about "household salvation," this was it!

For the first time, the Hinn home was transformed into "heaven on earth"! And the change was not temporary. It was a permanent work of the Spirit.

"IT'S ME!"

In May 1975, the Lord impressed me to do something I had never done before. By that time our services were being held in the beautiful fellowship hall of St. Paul's Anglican Church in downtown Toronto. During one meeting with several hundred people present, I looked across the audience and obeyed what the Lord was telling me. "Someone with a leg problem is being healed," I declared.

No one stood up, so I repeated the words. "Someone with a leg problem is being healed right now! Please stand up."

About a minute later a young woman with long red hair rose to her feet and began to make her way to the platform. "It's me!" she exclaimed. "I have been healed."

From that moment, God changed the direction of the ministry.

In service after service, people were being healed and delivered while the meeting was taking place. There were no more healing lines for the laying on of hands. The Lord began to do His work all across the auditorium—and so many were touched that there was not time to hear all of the testimonies.

The crowds grew and grew until we had to move Monday night meetings from the fellowship hall into the large sanctuary of St. Paul's Anglican Church—the same facility the Catacombs had used on Thursdays.

HEADING NORTH

"Benny, we're buying a plane ticket for you to go with us to Sault Sainte Marie"—a town in northwest Ontario, across the border from the Upper Peninsula of Michigan.

"What's going on up there?" I asked.

"There's a Full Gospel Businessmen's convention, and I've told the directors all about you," said my friend John Arnott.

Earlier that year John had been invited to the second meeting I conducted at Georges Vanier Secondary School, and had become a wonderful friend and great supporter of my ministry. As John later told me, "We knew that this was the anointing of God—it was something we had longed for."

When Kathryn Kuhlman came to Canada that year, John, his friend Sandy Fleming, and I volunteered to sing in the choir. We sat through the meeting and cried like babies—praying for the Spirit to be poured out on our lives.

John and his wife had the hearts of servants. They would drive me to meetings, help arrange the chairs, and he would even carry my luggage. We used to pray together as we drove the highways of Ontario, "Oh, Jesus, don't ever give us rest until we truly know You in all Your glory and power."

Many years later, John Arnott would lead a worldwide revival that became known as the "Toronto Blessing," and pastor the Toronto Airport Christian Fellowship.

In those days John was a successful entrepreneur who owned several farms and businesses in southern Ontario.

As we headed to the airport to fly to Sault Sainte Marie in September 1975, John said, "Benny, you need to know that the purpose of this trip is just to introduce you to the leadership of the Full Gospel Businessmen's Fellowship."

"You mean I'm not speaking?" I asked.

They confessed that there was great resistance from some of the leadership. In fact, one director told John, "No, we don't want a novice on the platform."

When we arrived at the Holiday Inn, John persuaded the conference chairman to let me give a short testimony.

"Friends," the leader of the service announced, "we are happy to have a young man from Toronto with us today, and we've asked him to share with you for the next few minutes."

I walked nervously to the platform, knowing hardly anyone in the building—and they certainly didn't know me. Then, just as I began, *wham!* The power of God hit that place like a hurricane of category five. For the next hour and a half, people were weeping, bodies were slain prostrate before the Lord, and miracles were taking place all over the room.

I knew instantly that this would not be my last visit to northern Canada.

NUTS AND BOLTS

The next afternoon, as the courtesy van was about to leave the Holiday Inn for the airport, the innkeeper stopped me and said, "Mr. Hinn, I would like you to meet one of our local ministers. This is Reverend Fred Spring."

Fred wasn't there for the businessmen's meeting; he had been attending a wedding reception in the same facility.

"I'm the pastor of the Elim Pentecostal Tabernacle, an Assemblies of God church here," he told me. Then this man—who had the most unique sideburns I had ever seen—said something that surprised even him. "I'd like you to come and speak in my church," he asked.

As Fred Spring told me later, "That was totally out of character for me. I was very picky about who I allowed to speak in my pulpit. Your name was vaguely familiar, and I had heard somewhere that you were a new evangelist involved in a healing ministry; I just felt led to ask you."

My response to Pastor Spring's invitation was, "I'll be there!"

That fall I returned to Sault Sainte Marie for a three-night crusade with Fred Spring. By Sunday night the people were lined up outside the Elim Pentecostal Tabernacle, waiting for a seat.

"Benny, my board is a little upset, but I want you to promise me you'll come back soon." Evidently, what was taking place in the services was far from typical. It left some old-timers shaking their heads.

Fred also told me that his church maintenance man was upset. "Can't you stop that guy from doing that?"

"Doing what?" Pastor Spring wanted to know.

"Well, having all those people being slain in the Spirit back in the pews," he replied.

"What's the problem?" Fred inquired.

"Some of the pews are coming loose from the floor and we have to drill out the bolts and replace them."

Fred just smiled. The work God was about to do in Sault Sainte Marie was more important than a few nuts and bolts.

CHAPTER 12

A JOURNEY OF MIRACLES

"Benny, I believe you need to return to northern Ontario at least three or four times a year," Fred Spring told me.

"Is that an invitation?" I chuckled.

Every time I visited Sault Sainte Marie for services the crowds grew—we had to move from the church to the White Pines Collegiate School auditorium.

I loved being in what we called "the north country" with Fred and his wife, Bette. Fred would borrow a four-wheel vehicle and we would travel as far north as we could go before running out of roads, often preaching in small churches.

I still smile when I think about the service we conducted in a place called Wawa. The wonderful pastor there had been an airplane pilot with Northland Missions, an Assemblies of God outreach in northern Canada. Unfortunately, the man had lost his arm in an accident. He fell off a pontoon and his arm was severed by the blade of the plane's propeller. Now, he wore a false arm and a claw.

We had a wonderful meeting in a church that was jammed to overflowing. And when the service was over, I wanted to thank everybody who had participated. "I think we ought to give the pastor a good hand," I said.

The people started laughing—including the minister—and I

didn't know why. I turned to Fred and said, "What did I say?"

"You asked them to give the pastor a good *hand*," he explained, chuckling.

It's one of the few times I've been embarrassed on the platform.

THE INDIAN CHIEF

During one of our trips up north, we held a meeting in the village of Spanish, Ontario, about 350 miles from Toronto. It was an Indian settlement.

The Indians are gracious people, yet quite stoic with stern faces and jutting chins. As I preached about God's miracle-working power, most of them just sat there, with their arms folded.

As I was about to conclude, a large Indian man stood to his feet and began slowly walking up the aisle with his wife and family. He walked with crutches. His face was expressionless as he continued to make his way to the front. As he came closer and closer, I waited for someone to stop him, but no one moved.

By the time he reached the front of the auditorium all eyes were focused on him.

"Sir, how can I help you?" I asked reluctantly as he walked up on the platform.

The man looked directly into my eyes and said, "You say that God heals."

"Yes, He does," I answered.

The Indian then proceeded to tell me what was wrong with him—and the list of ailments was long indeed. He went on to explain that he had been a cripple for twenty-eight years, and that his wife was ill with cancer. He also told us that his little girl suffered from a skin disease that caused severe bleeding on the skin's surface—and that the little baby his wife was carrying in her arms was also ill.

"You say God heals," he repeated. "Then prove it!"

As I looked at the man and his family standing before me, I knew there was nothing I could do for them. In desperation, I went to my knees—and asked all the preachers and a Catholic priest on the platform to join me. I lifted my hands and said, "Dear Jesus! I am not preaching *my* gospel. I am preaching *Your* gospel! This man is asking me to prove it. This is Your gospel— *You* prove it, dear Jesus!"

The words had barely left my lips when I heard a loud commotion. I opened my eyes to discover the entire family on the floor to the side of me—piled one on top of the other. They all went down under the power of the Holy Spirit.

I was amazed at what I saw.

"I've been healed!" shouted the father as he leaped to his feet. "I've been healed!" He was jumping up and down in joy and tears. Then he pulled back his little girl's sleeve, revealing skin as perfect as that of a baby. The skin disease had vanished and she was healed too!—and so were the wife and the little child.

As you can imagine, the audience was excited. Subdued and quiet just moments before, they were now praising God for the miracles that had taken place.

Revival came to that little community—and Jesus received all the praise.

To this day I am deeply moved every time I think of what God did in Spanish, Ontario.

ON BOARD

God obviously had a purpose in allowing me to meet Fred Spring in northern Canada. It was the beginning of a relationship with a man who was to play a vital role in the future of our ministry.

That same year, when we organized the Benny Hinn Evangelistic Association, Fred was not only a board member, but he also became executive director of the ministry. He flew to Toronto almost every Monday—on his day off—to handle administrative details and coordinate my speaking schedule.

The Lord surrounded me with some wonderful men of God. Our board included David Sturrie, Keith Elford, Frederick Browne—and Richard Green, a director of a major Toronto accounting firm, handled the finances.

During these days, I was conducting at least five services every week, not just in Canada; a growing number of invitations were also coming from the United States.

John Arnott, who spent considerable time in Florida, arranged my first speaking tour in the Sunshine State, including meetings at the Tabernacle Church in Melbourne, where Jamie Buckingham was the pastor. I also preached at a charismatic Episcopal church in Maitland and at the St. James Catholic Church in Orlando. Those anointed meetings opened many doors.

In Toronto, our Monday night miracles services moved to the spacious Evangelistic Center on York Mills Road. Every service was packed to capacity, with standing room only. Outside, the parking situation was described as "sheer mayhem." On any given Monday, you might find a busload of Catholics from Quebec, a group of Arabs from Egypt, or people who had driven from Michigan, New York, or Manitoba.

In our meetings I constantly told the crowd to turn their eyes toward our wonderful Jesus. I would tell them that God does not say, "I have healing." He always says, "I am the Lord who heals." Healing is a person. I preached that "the great secret to healing is the Lord Jesus."

I found that new believers—open to accepting everything God had for them, were also open and more ready to receive their healing. And they saw the power of the New Testament church in action.

"MR. PENTECOST"

At every turn, God was instructing me and shaping my ministry.

I had only been preaching for about one year when I was asked to be one of the speakers at a conference in Brockville, a town in eastern Ontario on the St. Lawrence River. It was there I met a gentleman whom I had come to regard as a giant in the faith—David DuPlessis.

Millions around the world knew and loved this man they called "Mr. Pentecost." He is the person who introduced the charismatic movement to the Catholic church. His teaching on the baptism of the Holy Spirit had been used mightily by God and had influenced countless lives.

The conference, held in a hotel, was organized by Maudie Phillips, a woman who worked with Kathryn Kuhlman.

Following a session with David DuPlessis, as I was walking down a hallway, Maudie called to me and asked, "Would you walk with David to his room?"

I was elated and thought, *What a privilege to be asked to walk this servant of God to his hotel room.*

Maudie introduced me to Dr. DuPlessis and left. I smiled at "Mr. Pentecost" as we walked along. I can still recall how neatly this rather short, white-haired man was dressed, carrying a dignified-looking briefcase. I was thrilled for the chance to be near such a man of God. Walking down the hallway, my mind was whirling with things I wanted to ask—but wasn't sure how.

Finally, deciding not to waste this perfect opportunity, I gathered my courage, took a deep breath, and asked, "Mr. DuPlessis, how can I please God?"

The moment those words left my lips, he stopped walking down the hallway, put his briefcase on the floor and turned toward me. Placing his thick, short finger on my chest, he pushed me back against the wall. Then he peered through his glasses, and in a serious tone of voice, said, "Don't even try." And he added, "It's not your ability; it's His ability in you."

With that he promptly said, "Good night," stepped back, picked up his briefcase, and disappeared into his room.

I just stood there, with my back still pressed against that wall—lost for words.

What did he mean? I wondered. I had expected a profound, lengthy answer from this spiritual giant, and all he said was, "Don't even try. It's not your ability; it's His ability in you."

It took me several years to fully comprehend the great lesson found in those words. I now know there is no need to attempt to please Him in my own strength. That would be futile; for He completed the work on the cross when He said, "It is finished!"

I have learned that all I have to do is surrender to the Holy Spirit—and He will do the rest. That's what David DuPlessis meant.

Later, Dr. DuPlessis and I became close friends and I had the opportunity to talk with him about the things of the Spirit. In fact, just before he passed away, I was privileged to work with him for a short time in association with my good friends Ronn Haus and Tommy Reid. He had a ministry that was called "John 17:21," which focused on forgiveness.

A CANCELED MEETING

In late November 1975, I received a phone call from Maudie Phillips. "Benny," she said, "I know you have wanted to meet Kathryn for some time and I have it all arranged. In fact, I have been telling her about your ministry. Can you be in Pittsburgh next Friday morning? She will be able to meet with you right after the service."

"Of course, I'll be there," I replied with great excitement. The idea that I would finally have the opportunity to meet Miss Kuhlman was thrilling. I was anxious to express my gratitude for the pivotal role she had played in my life.

I arrived early at First Presbyterian Church. As usual, people were lined up by the hundreds waiting for the doors to open. A few minutes later a staff member came to me and said, "I know you are here to meet with Miss Kuhlman after the service. However, she will not be here today. She is sick and has been taken to the hospital."

No one could remember anything like this happening before.

Kathryn *never* canceled a service. Moments later the entire waiting crowd was given the same message. The news was cause for great concern. They were stunned. In hushed whispers they asked one another, "I wonder how serious it really is?" "Do you think they will tell us more?"

There was no reason for me to stay. I left Pittsburgh and returned to Canada.

Three months later, on February 20, 1976, Kathryn Kuhlman died of a heart condition.

When the news of her death reached me, I buried my head in my hands and began to cry. Although I had never met her, Kathryn seemed like a member of my family. She had presented me with a banquet of spiritual food and her words had inspired me beyond measure. A flood of memories flashed across my mind and all I could do was fall to my knees and pray, "Lord, thank You for Miss Kuhlman. Thank You for using her to touch my life."

Many times, I've been asked, "Benny, tell me about Miss Kuhlman. What was she like?"

They are surprised when I say, "Oh, I never had the opportunity to meet Kathryn personally." Looking back on my journey to Pittsburgh, I believe what happened that day was in God's providence.

As I told members of my staff recently, had I met Kathryn it is possible that I would have forever believed she gave the anointing to me, or that God may have used her in some way to transfer it to me. No, the Lord wanted me to clearly understand that the anointing comes from Him, not from any person.

I firmly believe God uses His servants to influence us to walk in His ways—even to bring us into an atmosphere where miracles

Benny's mother and father, Clemence
and Constandi Hinn.

(Left to right) Benny's cousin Toufik,
his brother Chris, Benny, and his sister Rose.

Costandi Hinn with three of his sons,
(left to right) Benny, Willie, and Chris.

Benny's mother, Clemence (second from right),
with her two brothers and sister. That's Benny
standing in front of his mom.

Benny with some of his friends from
the Shekinah days in Europe in 1974.

Madame, Eleasha, and Joshua.

Suzanne and Benny at their wedding
on August 4, 1979.

Jessica (left) and Natasha with their dogs.

Preaching at a conference on
the Holy Spirit in Jerusalem.

Ministering in the early days in Canada
(with Fred Browne in the background).

Ministering at Calvary Assembly in Orlando
with Roy Harthern.

Breaking ground at Orlando Christian Center.
Three board members who assisted Benny greatly
in these early days were Floyd Mincy (holding
the microphone), Wes Benton, and
Tom Spence (far right in glasses).

With His Holiness Pope John Paul II.

Pastor Benny with the late King Hussein of Jordan.

Pastor Benny and Oral Roberts.

Sharing a moment with Paul and Jan Crouch.

Pastor Benny and his wife, Suzanne, at a crusade.

Evangelist Rex Humbard showing his affection for Benny, with Ronn Haus in the background (left).

Kathryn Kuhlman.

Jim Poynter ministering at a crusade.

With Dr. Lester Sumrall.

In Germany visiting the Lutheran Sisters of Mary, an order begun by Mother Basilea Schlink, whose ministry touched Pastor Benny's life greatly.

Joshua and Eleasha at a crusade.

(Left to right) Natasha, Eleasha, Jessica, and Joshua.

Suzanne, Jessica, and Natasha at a crusade.

Benny's mother, Clemence, holding the arm of Queen Rania of Jordan.

Preaching in Papua New Guinea.

The crowd of 300,000 in Papua New Guinea.

Some of the 500,000 people who
attended the crusade in Manila.

A crusade in Louisville, Kentucky. A typical monthly
crusade such as this will draw crowds of up to 20,000
for each service.

An artist's rendering of the new World Healing Center.

occur. The Lord did not give me any special power or gift through Kathryn Kuhlman, instead He used her to help me *find* the anointing.

MIRACLES AND MEDIA

Starting in 1976, the press in Canada began to take notice of our meetings. There were front-page stories of the "Miracle Rallies" we were conducting.

The *Toronto Globe and Mail* sent reporters Peter Whelan and Aubrey Wice to the service in Convocation Hall at the University of Toronto. Under a banner headline, "Faith Healing: The Power of Belief," they gave an account of the testimonies of healing. And they concluded the feature by quoting me: "I'm not interested in building up Benny Hinn. I'm not and never will be. Jesus is the One . . . to be built up and exalted. We want to reach souls for the Lord Jesus. I want to see souls, souls, souls, souls, souls. People, do you understand that?"

The *Toronto Star*, in a major feature, ran the headline "Does Faith Healing Really Work?" A reporter presented four case studies of people who had been healed in our services. He told about a shift worker at the GM plant in Oshawa who had cancer of the throat. "This week, following a checkup at the cancer clinic, he was told there is no trace of malignancy."

He also detailed the account of a Beaverton trucker: "A nonchurchgoer, who had suffered from congestive heart failure and slight emphysema (a lung disease) for seven years, was persuaded by friends to attend a healing crusade. 'I went to the doctor three days later, and he told me he could find nothing wrong,' he says. 'God must have done it.'"

What about their doctors? The reporter quoted one as saying, "Look, there are more things happening in this world than we know about."

Television stations began to film documentaries of what God was doing. The Canadian Broadcasting Corporation (CBC), Global TV, and the huge independent station in Toronto, Channel 9, produced news reports. The stories in the media were not critical accounts, but factual descriptions of what was taking place.

PETRIFIED IN PITTSBURGH

On February 20, 1977, I was invited to Pittsburgh to speak at a memorial service honoring Miss Kuhlman. The Carnegie Music Hall was filled.

I had been preaching for more than two years, yet I felt like a novice that night. While the film of her ministry was being shown, I looked out from behind the stage curtain and my knees began to buckle—my stomach was in knots. Most of these people did not know me, and had never before been in my meetings.

Jimmie McDonald, her longtime crusade soloist, introduced me and I was so nervous I couldn't speak. I simply led the audience in singing, "Jesus, Jesus, There's Just Something About That Name." They sang it over and over again.

After what seemed like an eternity, I finally threw my arms in the air and cried aloud, "I can't do it! Lord, I can't do it!"

At that precise moment I heard a voice deep inside me that said, *I'm glad you can't. Now I will.*

Instantly, the apprehension and fear vanished. My physical

body relaxed. I began to speak words I hadn't prepared, and the power of God began to touch people across the auditorium. It was a memorable, moving evening.

For the next three years, I held miracle services in Pittsburgh several times each year at the Carnegie Music Hall and the Soldiers and Sailors Memorial Hall, sponsored by the Kathryn Kuhlman Foundation.

In the year following Kathryn Kuhlman's passing, I was asked by her foundation to travel to cities across Canada and the United States for special miracle services. Jimmie McDonald sang, the film of Kathryn's Las Vegas meeting was shown, and I would minister. At Queensway Cathedral in Toronto, McCormick Place in Chicago, and in Vancouver, people were being healed during the *film,* even before I walked onto the platform. The powerful anointing God had placed on her life was still present in those meetings.

CONVERSATION IN A YELLOW CAB

In both 1976 and 1977 I was invited to speak at the Conference on the Holy Spirit in Jerusalem, sponsored by Logos International. It was my first time back to my homeland since we had emigrated eight years earlier. The burden I felt for the Middle East was overpowering. "Lord," I prayed, "somehow open the door so that I may one day return and preach Your message to the people of the Holy Land."

In both Canada and the United States, our ministry was expanding. On December 7, 1977, we held a three-year anniversary banquet at the Sheraton Center in Toronto. More than one thousand people attended.

The Lord was blessing the ministry greatly and some encouraged me to begin a television program. We contracted for a prime-time slot on a major station—Sunday nights at 10:00 P.M. following *60 Minutes*. The program was called, *It's a Miracle*.

Toronto was where I had been saved, healed, and touched by the mighty Spirit of God. The press had nothing but good news to report about the ministry, yet in my heart I felt I would soon be leaving the city. I prayed for the leading of the Holy Spirit.

I knew the Lord was directing me to establish an international ministry, I just didn't know where. Two years earlier, while riding in a Yellow Cab in Pittsburgh, I had a conversation with the Holy Spirit regarding this matter. He clearly showed me that the ministry "will touch the world."

I wondered, *Where will it be? New York? Los Angeles?* More than 90 percent of our ministry was taking place in the United States. I felt that's where He was leading, but the precise location was not clear.

Through some unexpected events, God was about to reveal His plan.

CHAPTER 13

"She's Going to Be Your Wife"

I was more than frustrated when I reached the airport check-in desk and was informed, "Mr. Hinn, your flight to Manila has been canceled."

It was the summer of 1978 and I was on my way to attend a John 17:21 Conference in Singapore headed by David DuPlessis. There were a number of minister friends I was looking forward to seeing—including Ronn Haus, who at that time was working with David.

I booked a different flight that was to stop in Hong Kong, Thailand, then on to Singapore—making the trip much longer. I barely arrived before the final session of the conference. To make matters worse, my speaking schedule was so tight I had to return to Toronto almost immediately.

There was a surprise waiting for me on the return flight. Roy Harthern was on board. He was a transplanted Englishman, and the pastor of one of America's largest Assemblies of God churches at the time—Calvary Assembly in Orlando, Florida. I had been a guest speaker in his pulpit (preaching five times on one Sunday) and it was such a joy to see him. "Let's ask the stewardess to change our seating so we can spend this time together," Roy suggested.

We hadn't been in the air long before he pulled out his wallet and proudly said, "Let me show you my girls." I had not met his entire family since his twin daughters were away at college when I was in Orlando. They were attending Evangel College, an Assemblies of God liberal arts school in Springfield, Missouri.

He showed me the photos of his three daughters, one by one, telling me their names and a little bit about them. He held out one picture and said, "Now this is Suzanne"—and I leaned over to get a better look.

Instantly, something inside was saying, *She's going to be your wife*. It wasn't an audible voice, yet it was unmistakable. *She's going to be your wife*.

"Can I look at that picture again?" I asked Roy. And I said to myself, "What a beautiful young lady."

At the same time I thought, *Lord, this is not the time to tell me about a wife*.

HE HANDED ME THE PHONE

During that summer I was facing the first real crisis since launching our ministry. Because of the enormous cost of the television programs in Canada, we were under a burden of tremendous debt—something I never thought would happen. Although we had ended the telecasts, the bills we still owed were staggering.

On the plane, Roy Harthern got out his schedule book and said, "Benny, let's lock down a time you can be back in Orlando this fall." We set the date and I returned to his church in September.

One afternoon during the crusade I was in Roy's office when he dialed the number of his daughter's dorm room at Evangel

College. In the middle of their conversation, he said, "Suzanne, there is someone here who would like to say hello"—and he handed the phone to me.

"Suzanne, this is Benny Hinn," I said, in my warmest, friendliest voice. "I've heard some wonderful things about you. In fact your dad showed me your picture while we were flying back from Singapore together. I hope I can meet you sometime."

She responded by saying, "I've heard great things about you too."

I didn't know it at the time, but her father had already shown Suzanne my picture during the summer and said, "What do your think of him? He may be your type."

Suzanne's response was, "Whatever God wants!" And she didn't think any more about it.

In October, while I was in Canada, Suzanne came home to Florida for a mid-semester school break. One afternoon, while riding in the car, her mother, Pauline, related a conversation she had with Suzanne's grandmother, a woman of prayer from Cardiff, Wales. "Your grandmother asked the Lord, 'Who will Suzanne marry?' And the Lord told her, 'Benny Hinn'"—and that dear woman had never even met me!

Nineteen-year-old Suzanne brushed it off as just a comment from someone who was getting quite elderly and could simply be confused. Plus, she was interested in her studies and wasn't about to get into a serious relationship.

MY KNEES WERE WEAK

As Christmas was approaching, I telephoned Roy Harthern and asked, "What would you think about my coming down and spending a few days with you during the holiday season?"

"Wonderful," he replied. "Can you be here for Christmas?"

I had never spent Christmas away from my family before, yet something was drawing me south, and it wasn't the Florida sun. I still remembered the photo I had seen on the plane and the reaction I felt in my heart.

Suzanne returned home from college for the holidays and was informed that an evangelist—the same one she had spoken with on the phone—would be spending the holidays at their home. "Just treat him like part of the family," Pauline told her girls.

When I arrived at the Hartherns' on Saturday, Suzanne wasn't there. She had gone ahead to the home of some people from the church where we had all been invited for dinner. She told me much later, "I didn't want to seem anxious to meet you."

Just after I walked into that home, Suzanne came into the living room from the kitchen. I looked into her beautiful bluish-green eyes and my knees became weak!

A COCOA BEACH CONFIRMATION

Christmas was on Monday, and the Hartherns opened their hearts to me—and had my name on presents under the tree. After dinner, I said to Suzanne, "I have some friends in Cocoa Beach I'd like to visit this afternoon. Would you care to go with me?"

"Sure. Why not?" she replied in a tone that said, "I'm just going to be polite."

I drove to the home of Maxine and Harry LaDuke, a wonderful Christian couple I met the first time I was in Florida speaking at Jamie Buckingham's church. Maxine was a very godly woman—an intercessor.

We hadn't been in their home two minutes when Maxine pulled me aside and said, "Benny, that's your wife! When you walked in, there was an anointing on both of you!" To me, it was another confirmation of what I already felt.

"I'M GOING TO SURPRISE YOU"

During these days Suzanne and I had some wonderful conversations about what it means to live the Christian life. More and more I was impressed by her simplicity and purity.

You need to understand that I had set extremely high standards for the woman I would marry—I prayed for someone who had never touched a cigarette, never kissed a guy, and was still a virgin. Suzanne was meeting every expectation. Even more important, I was falling in love.

On Thursday I flew to San Jose, California, for year-end services at a large church pastored by Kenny Forman. And before leaving I asked Suzanne if she had a picture I could take with me. She found a wallet-size school photo.

Ronn Haus met me at the airport and asked me something that was becoming his standard joke, "Well, Benny, have you found a girlfriend yet?"

"I'm going to surprise you, Ronn," I replied. "Actually, I like Roy Harthern's daughter." I proudly showed him the photo.

Back in Orlando, Suzanne, her sisters, and mother began something that had become an annual tradition. They entered into a time of fasting and prayer to seek God's will for the year ahead.

Suzanne told me later that she began to feel something was happening between us, and prayed, "Lord, if this is You, confirm it to me. Have Benny call me today."

Ronn played a trick on me that day, dialing my room and telling me to call Suzanne, stating, "She phoned me and asked for you to call."

So I did—and we had a marvelous conversation.

The Lord used Ronn's little ploy to confirm again to Suzanne this was His will.

A TOUGH TEST

I was so taken with Suzanne that I asked the Hartherns if I could fly back and stay a few more days. During the time we were together, I put out "fleeces" to see if this was truly the girl I should marry, and every fleece was answered. I thought, *Is this just coincidence, or does God really want me to marry this young lady?*

Then I tried one last sign—a rather difficult one.

On Monday, New Year's Day, seated in the plane on my way back to Florida, I had a talk with God. I said, "If she really is to be my wife, have her say to me when I get back, 'I've made you a cheesecake.'" That was the most unusual test I could think of.

Suzanne met me at the Orlando airport, and the first words out of her mouth were, "Benny, I've made you a cheesecake." Then she added, "Don't expect too much. I've never made a cheesecake before!"

Since Suzanne was preparing to return to Evangel College I knew I had little time to lose.

"THIS WON'T TAKE LONG"

On Friday the Hartherns were up early, getting ready for a prayer meeting at the church called "Intercessors for America."

Roy had already left the house and Pauline was getting ready to leave.

When I asked, "Can I talk with you?" Pauline replied, "I'm sure you want to speak with me about Suzanne," making it easy for me. She thought I was going to ask permission to date their daughter.

Knowing she was in a hurry to leave, I said, "This won't take long."

In that room, alone where no one could hear, I must have stunned her when I said, "I want to marry Suzanne. I am in love with her." Then I added, "I've had a long list of things I am looking for in a wife, and your daughter meets every one."

"Well, well," she said in her crisp British accent, hesitating, "you really need to speak with her father, and he has already left for the prayer meeting. You'll have to talk with him when that's over."

Suzanne got dressed and went to the church with me—not knowing this conversation had even taken place.

When Pauline arrived at the church, she asked her husband to lead the prayer meeting, "My mind just wouldn't be on the service," she told him.

"What is it?" Roy wanted to know.

Pauline replied, "If I told you now, you would be distracted too."

After the prayer meeting, I went into Roy Harthern's office and after a short conversation I came right to the point. I said, "Roy, I would like to marry your daughter."

I knew his answer was "yes" when he smiled, pulled out his calendar and said, "When do you think the wedding should take place?" We both had extremely busy schedules.

Then he said, "Have you talked with Suzanne about this?"

"Well, not really," I sheepishly replied.

Immediately, Roy found Suzanne in the building and asked her to come to his office. In front of the two of them I asked, "Will you marry me?"

I was overjoyed when she accepted on the spot.

SUZANNE'S SECRET

That night Suzanne told me, "Benny, since I was raised in a pastor's home, I knew from the time I was very young that I wanted to give my life to ministry. I felt deep down inside that I would some day marry a preacher." And she told me another secret, "Since I was a little girl I knew the man I would marry would have dark hair, dark eyes, and an olive complexion. Benny, you are that man God has for me."

On Saturday morning we went to a local jewelry store and I bought her a diamond ring and slipped it on her finger right in the store.

A few nights later, my father and my brother Sammy flew down from Toronto to be at the engagement dinner. The noted Bible teacher Derek Prince, who was speaking the next day at Calvary Assembly, was a special guest.

When the announcement was made to the congregation on Sunday morning, the whole church erupted in applause—and there was a prophecy given that we would have a fruitful ministry together.

The Hinn-Harthern wedding was set to take place August 4, 1979.

"LET'S TALK"

Before I left Orlando, after an evening meal with the Harderns, Roy asked me to join him in their family room for a conversation. "Let's talk," he said.

Since I was about to become his son-in-law, I supposed there were things he wanted to know. "Tell me about yourself," he began as we sat facing each other.

Immediately, I started telling him about my family, and everything that seemed important. Of course, I didn't want to talk about the fact that because of our television project, our ministry was saddled with an enormous debt. I thought, *If I mention that, he might have second thoughts about the man who is about to marry his daughter.*

A few minutes into the conversation he brought up the subject of tithing, and I began to squirm. Yes, I had given to ministries as I felt led, but I was not a strict tither in those days—and Roy was quick to sense that fact.

He leaned toward me and said, "Never forget this, Benny. The law of giving is a fixed law you cannot change."

At that point I shared with him the weight of the financial burden I was carrying. I asked him, "What should I do?"

"Start paying God's bills," he quickly replied.

I said, "Roy, you don't understand. I don't have enough money to pay *my* bills."

Ignoring my words, he continued, "Benny, if you will pay God's bills, He will pay yours."

Two days later, Suzanne flew to Springfield, Missouri, to retrieve her belongings from the Evangel College dorm.

I caught a plane for Toronto—with Roy Harthern's words still echoing in my ears: "If you will pay God's bills, He will pay yours." I knew God was speaking to me.

I drove straight from the airport to our ministry office, about ten minutes away. As soon as I greeted my secretary I said, "Marian, get the checkbook out."

"What for?" she asked.

"Just get it out," I repeated. She retrieved the ministry checkbook and opened it on her desk.

"I want you to send a check for $1,000 to . . ." and with that I directed her to send specific amounts to a number of ministries and mission organizations. She became so nervous her hand started to shake as she wrote.

After she had completed two or three checks, Marian stopped and asked, "What are you doing?"

"I'm just obeying God," I told her.

"Are you sure God is talking to you?" she wanted to know.

"Absolutely," I said emphatically. "Absolutely."

Finally, Marian put down her pen and said, "You can't do this. You're going to be out of money soon and the ministry will be bankrupt." Then she looked down at the list and said, "I don't understand. These are not people to whom you owe any money."

"I know," I responded. "That's money I owe God, so let's obey Him."

A BEWILDERED BOARD

Earlier that day, flying to Toronto, I calculated that I owed God more than I owed the television station, and I was determined to obey.

Marian was still trembling when she had written the last check.

Then, when I went into another office, she phoned all the board members—who now numbered nine.

That same afternoon they gathered at the office for an emergency meeting. "What are you doing?" they demanded to know.

I replied, "I'm obeying God."

"But you're in debt. You can't do that," they objected. "We have bills to pay."

Without batting an eye, I said, "I'm obeying God. I'm paying God's bills."

Our CPA spoke up and said, "This ministry will be finished today if you do this." Then he began naming our creditors.

I continued, "God told me through one of His servants that I am to pay Him first."

Baffled, some of my board members resigned.

Then Fred Browne, a wonderful Christian who owned a home improvement company, said, "Are you sure God spoke to you?"

"Yes," I said with absolute confidence.

"Well, if God spoke to you, I'll stick with you."

"Thank you," I responded.

"Me too," echoed Fred Spring.

That same week, money miraculously began pouring into our ministry. There were handwritten notes attached to many of the checks, "The Lord told me to send this to you."

Within a few short months all of our bills had been paid—and we have never stopped tithing.

WHITE TUXEDOS

With the surprising events that transpired in December and January, I had no more questions regarding the new location for the Benny Hinn Evangelistic Association. In the spring of 1979 I moved to Orlando.

During these months I still kept a hectic schedule, yet I spent every moment possible with my bride-to-be. We flew to Toronto and my family opened their arms to her.

The wedding on August 4 was everything I imagined—and more.

Pauline Harthern wrote a special ceremony that was a combination of traditional English and American weddings—with a Middle Eastern blessing. I forgot some of the lines of my vows, but Suzanne just smiled.

Suzanne's twin sister, Leanne, was the maid of honor, and my younger sister Mary was a bridesmaid along with Suzanne's sister Elizabeth. Suzanne's cousins flew in from England and all of my brothers, plus Suzanne's brother, were part of the ceremony—looking spiffy in their white tuxedos. My niece Tina, Rose's daughter, was the flower girl.

The next day, as we were flying together over the Pacific Ocean, I thought about how far the Lord had brought me—Jaffa, Toronto, Orlando, and now to Hawaii for our honeymoon.

CHAPTER 14

A CORONATION DAY

Our first year of married life was like a whirlwind. Suzanne and I were in services from Buffalo to Anaheim—plus Sweden, Canada, England, Germany, and two journeys to Israel. And our daily radio program was being heard in major cities including Los Angeles, Detroit, Phoenix, Tulsa, Denver, Miami, and Orlando.

Like every married couple, we had some adjustments to make. Although Suzanne was determined to be a submissive wife, she revealed her strong will when it was necessary. I realized I had to soften some of my Middle Eastern attitudes or there would have been a clash of cultures.

"I have some wonderful news," she told me in the fall of 1981. "The doctor says I am pregnant." I was thrilled beyond words.

Our first daughter, Jessica, was born March 25, 1982. What an exciting time that was. She became the little princess of our home.

IT WAS SCARY

Most of the meetings I conducted in those years were in churches. We didn't travel with a team—it was just Suzanne and myself, flying from city to city. With the responsibility of a child, however, she stayed close to home.

Our Orlando family grew even larger when my parents

moved south from Canada—along with some of my brothers.

My father's thoughts of an early retirement were shattered in September 1982. While lifting a box at his home he felt a strange, uncomfortable sensation—like something tearing in his lungs. It was scary, and he knew that something was wrong.

He made an appointment with a physician and after a series of tests, the doctor gave him some dreadful news. "Mr. Hinn," he said, "I have to tell you that you have lung cancer."

My father hadn't been seriously ill a day in his life; however, he had been a heavy smoker, and this was the result.

He could not believe it, and told my mom, "That doctor is crazy. I need to talk with someone else."

When I heard the news, I was devastated. I called the physician and asked, "Sir, how can you be so sure that my father has lung cancer?"

"It showed in the blood test," he replied.

I said, "Daddy, you need to get a second opinion. Go to your doctor in Canada and have him check you. He's known you a long time." Immediately, he began making preparations for the journey.

I was preaching a crusade at First Assembly of God in Pensacola, Florida, keeping in touch with my mother by phone.

"Benny," she told me one night, "your father is not doing very well. We're leaving for Toronto tomorrow."

I did everything in my power to find a way to Orlando, but it looked impossible. The flight I planned to be on was canceled. I finally found the pilot of a private single-engine airplane who agreed to take me to the Orlando airport.

The plane landed just as the commercial jet carrying my father was taking off. I had missed him.

Almost as quickly as our family physician in Toronto examined my father, he made arrangements to have him admitted to the hospital.

Later, I talked with him on the phone and could tell by his voice that he was losing his strength.

When I reached Toronto he was already in intensive care, plugged into a respirator and an intravenous feeding unit. He could not talk to me or see me because of the heavy drugs he had been given. However, when I walked into the room he heard me and knew I was there.

We prayed that God would restore his body, yet I looked up to God and said, "If You won't heal him, please take him home, Lord."

Two nights later, as I was sleeping at my sister's home, I had a dream and saw my father. He was beaming with joy, his face was aglow.

That same day, when I awoke, there was a phone call from the hospital. "Mr. Hinn, we regret to inform you that your father has passed away." He died of lung cancer at the age of fifty-eight.

There was a peace and assurance in my heart that he was now in heaven. I thought once more of that night in 1975 when, at two o'clock in the morning in the living room of our home, Costandi Hinn gave his heart to Christ.

ONLY A SHELL

Since most of our relatives still attended the Greek Orthodox church in Toronto, my mother thought it would be fitting that the funeral service of her beloved husband be held in that church.

Mom visited the priest and said, "I want you to be in charge of the first part of the service, and I want my son Benny to speak when you have finished."

When the priest protested, Mother said, "This is our service and that's the way I want it." He reluctantly agreed.

Three hundred friends and relatives gathered in the ornate sanctuary of the Greek Orthodox church, and my father's casket was placed before the altar.

After the traditional religious ceremonies were concluded, the priest nodded for me to come to the front.

I opened my Bible and began to preach a simple message of salvation. I told the assembled crowd, "My father is not in that casket—that is only his shell." I read the Scripture that "to be absent from the body is to be present with the Lord."

At one point I walked over to the casket and began pounding on it. "My daddy is not in here!" I declared. "He is not here! He's gone to be with Jesus!"

Every person in that sanctuary was staring at me. I glanced over at the priest and could tell by his expression that he was quite nervous. He didn't know how to react.

I then called my mother, Suzanne, my brothers, and my sisters to the front. We gathered around the casket and began to worship the Lord. Our eyes were closed and our hands were outstretched toward heaven. Spontaneously, we began to sing, "Then sings my soul, my Savior God to Thee, How great Thou art! How great Thou art!"

When I opened my eyes and looked at the congregation, the people were stunned. Some were crying. At that moment I felt led to give an altar call. "If you want to know this same Jesus I have been talking about, I would like to pray with you right now," I said.

Several friends of my father gave their hearts to Jesus that day—including two of my cousins.

It was a coronation day!

RALPH PRAYED

I felt the loss of my father deeply. In the last years of his life we had become extremely close. It was a loving relationship of mutual respect, made strong by the bonds of Calvary.

Now that he was gone my heart was heavy.

The week after the funeral I stood behind the pulpit at Melodyland in Anaheim, California, and found it difficult to preach. After the service, riding in the car with my friend Pastor Ralph Wilkerson and his wife, Allene, I said, "Ralph, I need you to pray for me. I am really feeling the loss of my dad."

Right in that car, Ralph began to pray out loud—and the presence of the Lord came on me that night like a radiant sunrise. Driving down the freeway, we were singing and praising the Lord!

I thank God for people like the Wilkersons whom God has sent into my life at special moments.

A FLIGHT TO PHOENIX

On the day we moved the headquarters of our ministry to Orlando, God began to deal with me about opening a church—a center of healing and hope that would be the home base of a worldwide outreach.

Personally, I fought the idea. "Lord, can't I just keep walking through the doors You are opening? Do I really need the responsibility of pastoring a congregation?"

It seemed that every time I prayed, the call from the Lord became stronger.

At one point I said, "Lord, if You want me to build a church, why does it have to be in Orlando? Why not some other city?" I even thought seriously about moving to Phoenix, Arizona.

I decided that on my next trip to the West Coast, I would stop in Phoenix and survey the city. A few weeks later that's where I was headed.

On the plane I was seated next to a gentleman from Orlando— a businessman who happened to be Episcopalian. After we conversed for a few minutes he asked, "What do you do for a living?"

When I told him, he said, "Do you have a card?"

"No," I replied, "but I have one of my newsletters." And on the back of it was my schedule.

He looked it over and said, "I don't know why I'm telling you this, but you need to settle down and let some of these people come to you."

I told him, "I'm flying to Phoenix today because I'm thinking about moving my headquarters there."

In strong words, he told me, "There's no comparison. Orlando is going to be booming in the next few years. That's where you need to be."

"GOD SENT HIM"

After a short stay in Phoenix I continued on to San Jose to minister for my friend Kenny Forman, who received a word from the Lord for me, saying, "If you don't start a church in Orlando you will be missing God."

From there I went to Tampa, Florida, and the Lord gave me

an almost identical message through another man. Then I spoke for my dear friend Tommy Reid in Buffalo, New York, who said, "You must obey God and start a church in Orlando."

Meanwhile, my father-in-law, Roy Harthern, resigned as pastor of the megachurch Calvary Assembly, in Orlando. People were telling me, "Benny, this certainly leaves open the doors for you to begin a new church—and you won't be in competition with someone in the family."

It seemed that every time I prayed, I could see the skyline of Orlando. I saw the faces of people in that city who were hungry for more of God. "Lord, what are You saying to me?"

I said to Suzanne, "I can't shake this thing. The Lord is really dealing with me about starting a church here. It won't go away."

One night after earnestly praying, I stood to my feet, looked up to heaven and said, "Okay, Lord, I'm going to rent a large auditorium and have a one-night service. If You fill that building for me, I'll know it is of You, and I will start a church."

"MIRACLE LIFE CENTER"

In late fall, 1982, we booked the Tupperware Auditorium near Kissimmee, just outside of Orlando. Not only was the building packed, it was one of the greatest meetings we had ever experienced in the city.

For the next few months we began making plans to begin a church that would make an impact on the entire central Florida region. We leased the Youth for Christ building on Gore Street in downtown Orlando and announced that Sunday, March 20, 1983, the "Miracle Life Center" would convene its first service. More than four hundred attended.

I had no idea how long I would pastor a church in Orlando. It could be for a year, five years, ten years—or even more. My prayer was, "Lord, I'm just obeying You."

In the late 1970s and early 1980s I preached many times in Jacksonville, Florida, at a wonderful church pastored by Paul Zink. He was leaving about that same time, and an outstanding musical group in his church decided to move to Orlando and become part of our ministry. My brother Willie, who was assisting me at Miracle Life Center at the time, was delighted. He later married one of the young ladies in the singing group.

The church began with Sunday afternoon services, but soon we were having Sunday morning, Sunday night, and Wednesday night meetings.

In the mid-1970s I began appearing as a guest on *Praise the Lord,* the flagship program of the Trinity Broadcasting Network. Paul and Jan Crouch, hosts of the telecast, had given me a standing invitation to be on the program anytime I was in southern California.

When Paul Crouch, president of TBN, heard that I was starting a church, he said, "Benny, why don't you video your Sunday services? I'll put you on the network free. All you'll have to pay is the local production costs and send us the tapes."

Immediately, we assembled a television crew and began filming the Sunday morning services from our Gore Street location. From 1983 to 1990 they carried the program every week—free.

I meet people almost every week whose lives were touched by those Sunday telecasts.

Week by week, word of what God was doing at Miracle Life

Center began to spread. And Satan must have heard it too.

Just two months after we began our ministry in Orlando, tragedy struck. In one unexpected moment, Suzanne and I were being hurled headlong into the face of death.

CHAPTER 15

THE CRASH

"We're in trouble!" said the pilot.

Those words woke me from my sleep. We were flying in a small, single-engine, private aircraft at 11,000 feet, returning to Orlando from Naples, Florida, in May 1983. There were six of us on board. It was one o'clock in the morning and the sky was pitch black.

"I think we are out of fuel," said the concerned pilot as the engine sputtered and stopped.

Suzanne was seated next to me. She was doing her best to remain calm, yet I could tell she was extremely nervous—by the pain her nails were inflicting on my arm as she gripped it tightly.

The next few intense minutes seemed to be an eternity. We were both frightened—I could feel my heart pounding against my rib cage.

I thought, *God in heaven, I could be with You any minute.* Then I began to ask myself, Am I ready?

At such a moment you have no idea how powerful that question becomes. My answer left no room for doubt. Yes, I was ready.

Suddenly, as the plane was falling and the pilot was anxiously searching for an emergency landing site, my mind flashed back to an event that had happened eight months earlier.

SATAN'S SCHEME

The previous September, at the funeral home just before my father's memorial service, the director approached me and said, "Reverend Hinn, we need a necktie for your father. Could you get one for him?"

Immediately, I took off the tie I was wearing and gave it to the mortician. Later, after the funeral service, I was standing before the coffin at the cemetery. As they were lowering the casket of my dear father into the ground, something happened that I had almost dismissed from my memory. But now, as the plane was free-falling, I remembered it all too clearly.

As the pallbearers continued lowering the coffin, something unusual began taking place. I had given my necktie to my father, yet suddenly I felt a tightening around my neck—as if my own necktie were choking me. At the same time I heard a voice say, "I will kill you within one year."

I immediately responded out loud and said, "No, you won't!" I knew that when Satan speaks I had better talk back, even if people were around.

I looked toward heaven and said: "Lord Jesus, the devil can't do that!" Instantly I heard the comforting assurance of the Holy Spirit. He spoke only two words but they were all I needed. The Spirit said, "He won't."

Now, on the plane, those words of Satan took on an ominous tone: "I'm going to kill you within one year!" Thankfully, I also recalled the voice of the Holy Spirit.

It took just a second for the entire scene to flash through my mind. Then the peace of God embraced me and I heard the voice of the Lord again tell me: "All is well!"

I turned to Suzanne and the frightened passengers and assured them, "Don't worry. We're going to be all right!"

Usually I'm quite excitable, yet at that moment I became totally calm. Without the roar of the engine it became eerily quiet in that plane. The pilot spotted an airstrip near Avon Park, Florida, and did his best to maneuver the troubled craft to the runway. With no power it became impossible—and he missed it.

The plane crashed.

THE HAND OF AN ANGEL

We smashed into a tree and the small aircraft rolled over four times. It was totally destroyed—the wheels were ripped off and hung in a tree. The fuselage was so damaged that an onlooker would wonder if there could be even one survivor. The engine was torn from its housing and we were upside down.

The door of the plane had disappeared and I crawled out to realize that there was not a scratch on my body. I was untouched. In the darkness, disoriented, I began to run in circles for help, not knowing where I was, or what direction to head. I concluded we were in the middle of a farm. Then I thought, *What in the world am I doing? I had better get back and help Suzanne and the others.*

I ran to the plane to discover that I was the only one uninjured. The pilot was making horrible sounds as I tried to pull him out.

In the darkness I saw Suzanne. Her leg was hanging out of the door. There was no movement and I wondered if she was seriously injured. Desperate to get her out of the plane, I began to pull, and as I did, it felt as if Suzanne's leg was broken. I soon discovered her arm was also mangled.

Miraculously, not one person was killed in the crash. As the ambulance raced to the crash site—and it seemed to take forever—I began to cry, "Lord, the devil wanted to kill all of us, but Your angel was with us!"

Later I learned at that exact moment a woman in California was awakened from her sleep. She recounted the story to me of how God awoke her and said, "Benny Hinn and his wife are in danger! Pray!" She told me, "Young man, the devil wanted to snuff out your life!"

How well I knew it.

I also knew that the Lord was not finished with Suzanne and me. The Holy Spirit had given me the assurance that God's protection was on our lives for a reason.

A COLORFUL BIBLE

I believe that establishing a ministry in Orlando at that time in my life was divinely ordered. Not only were people's lives being miraculously touched, I was challenged to delve into God's Word day after day to prepare myself for the services. All across the auditorium, people had their Bibles open, taking notes on every message.

On several occasions, people have looked at my personal Bible—the one I study and preach from—and commented,

"That's the most colorful Bible I've ever seen. What are all those markings?"

From my Toronto days, I have made it a habit to color-code every important Scripture I read in the Word. In fact I always have seven pencils with me when I study the Bible—each with a different color. Here's how I mark the Scriptures:

Red: Promises.
Blue: Teaching—or learning.
Brown: Very important.
Orange: Commandments.
Green: Prophecies and their fulfillment.
Purple: Prayer.
Yellow: Things to especially remember.

Sometimes I mix two colors. For example: Brown and green tell me this is a very important prophecy.

In addition to adding color to the Scriptures, I use a wide-margin King James Version of the Bible—with room for writing notations.

"IT'S YOURS!"

"What are we going to do?" I asked those who were helping me build the new ministry. "We're out of space."

The church was less than four months old and there was standing room only at Miracle Life Center. With great urgency we began searching for land on which to build a permanent facility.

We soon found a large piece of property, strategically located on Forest City Road, in north Orlando. It was on a lake—Lake Lovely.

I remember the day I walked that property end to end, praying, "Lord, I claim this land for You. I claim it in Jesus' name!"

I met the elderly woman who owned the land and said, "God told me this property would be ours."

That didn't seem to impress her. "Well, Reverend," she commented, "we already have another buyer."

"I'm only telling you what the Lord instructed me," I replied.

What I failed to mention was that we didn't have a dime to pay for it.

A few weeks later I returned to the woman's house and reiterated, "God told me this property would be ours."

This time, her response totally changed. She replied, "Well, if you can come up with the down payment, I'll sell you the land. Then she made a confession. "Young man, let me tell you something you may find quite interesting."

"What is it?" I wanted to know.

"Well," she began, "before my husband passed away, he made me vow that the only thing to be built on this property would be a church." Then she said, "It's yours!"

Needless to say, the following Sunday there was glory on Gore Street.

"LET'S GO!"

A few days later, I was in Miami, Florida, speaking at a church that was started by my friend Bill Swad, a dynamic Christian businessman who owned several automobile dealerships in

Ohio. After the morning service, Bill said, "Benny, there's a man in the hospital I feel we need to go and pray for. Will you go with me?"

To be honest, I didn't feel like going. It was an extremely hot and humid day, I was exhausted from the service, and felt I needed to rest. Bill, however, kept insisting that we go and pray for this gentleman.

Reluctantly, I accompanied Bill to the man's hospital room. He was on a dialysis machine—tubes everywhere. His name was Floyd Mincy.

"Floyd, this is Benny Hinn," said Bill. "I've asked him to come and pray for you."

Mr. Mincy nodded in agreement.

I quickly prayed for him, asking the Lord to heal him—and subtly gave Bill signals that implied, "Let's go!"

Three weeks later, Floyd and his wife, Maryana, attended our Sunday morning service at Miracle Life Center in Orlando. Floyd testified how the Lord had healed him, saying, "The moment you walked out of that hospital room I was completely healed by the power of God. Completely!"

During the service I talked about the vision to construct a church on the new property—and I shared my passion to reach lost souls for the Lord. When the meeting concluded, Floyd and Maryana came to me and said, "Pastor Benny, the Lord told us to assist you in what He has called you to do."

It was Floyd and Maryana who later helped the church put a large sum of money on the new property.

In spite of my hurried prayer in that hospital room, the Lord was faithful.

God continued to bless the church through the lives of many

outstanding individuals—people like Wes Benton and Emil
Tanis, early board members and great supporters of the ministry.

On Sunday, November 17, 1983, we had a groundbreaking
service at the new property and unveiled plans for the new
Orlando Christian Center.

TWO GREAT EVENTS

Since our Sunday morning services were being televised by
TBN nationally and via satellite to several foreign countries,
there were visitors in practically every service. "We didn't just
come to Orlando to see Mickey Mouse," they would tell us.
"We watch you every week on television and couldn't wait to
get here."

I will always remember 1984 because of two great events that
took place. First, on May 1, Suzanne and I became the proud
parents of our second child—a beautiful little girl we named
Natasha.

Second, we moved into the new 2,300-seat auditorium on
Forest City Road. It was the beginning of a great spiritual adventure for me, for my family, and for the thousands of lives that
have been saved, healed, and delivered because we obeyed God.

I had no way of knowing that "OCC," as it was called,
would be the launching pad for something even greater that
God was preparing.

CHAPTER 16

A MANDATE FROM HEAVEN

"Benny, I have some outstanding people coming to work with me and you need to meet them," said my brother Henry, who, at the time, was a traveling evangelist. It was July 1986.

After a Wednesday night service at our church, Henry introduced me to Dave and Sheryl Palmquist, who had moved to Orlando to be the administrators of his ministry. Previously, this talented couple had been staff members at Soul's Harbor Church in Minneapolis, Minnesota, and at the Cathedral of Tomorrow in Akron, Ohio.

After the first time I heard Sheryl play the piano and organ, I asked her to be part of the musical team at Orlando Christian Center. They became faithful members of the church. Then in February 1987, when Dave Palmquist and my brother Henry were driving me to the airport, I turned to Dave and said, "You know, you are to be a pastor at OCC—I have already discussed this with Henry and he gave his blessing." The Lord confirmed this to Dave's heart and he joined our staff the next month.

"WHAT ARE YOU DOING IN FLORIDA?"

A few weeks later I made a telephone call to a gentleman who had played a pivotal role in my early Canada days—Fred Spring, the pastor at Sault Sainte Marie who had been a founding member of my board.

Fred had resigned from the church in Canada and, after pastoring in Michigan and Ohio, moved to Lakeland, Florida—uncertain of his future. I still don't know how his new telephone number came to my attention, but I called him and said, "Fred, what are you doing in Florida? I was on my way to the airport and felt led of the Holy Spirit to call you."

Delighted, Fred responded, "Benny, it is so good to hear your voice."

After a few pleasantries, I told him, "I feel in my spirit you are to join our staff in Orlando. You don't have to answer me right now."

He and his wife, Bette, were in shock. However, twelve days later, after praying about the matter, Fred and Bette joined the staff.

"I KNOW JUST THE PERSON"

That same year I was in California appearing on the Trinity Broadcasting Network. A guest that night was the bass singer Big John Hall. During a break in the program I turned to John and said, "Don't leave after the program. I need to talk with you."

When we finally spoke, I asked, "John, in your travels have you come across anyone who would be a great minister of music for our church?" We were looking for a person who had the Spirit of God on his life and someone who could take our music program to a higher level.

John smiled and answered, "I think I know just the person.

His name is Jim Cernero. He was the minister of music at First Assembly in North Hollywood, California, and is now at a church on the East Coast. You should give him a call."

Big John Hall found the phone number and I called Jim Cernero the next morning. "Can you and your wife fly to Orlando this weekend?" I asked. Jim was rather surprised, especially since he had seen me on TBN the previous night.

"Yes," he responded. "We'll be there."

That Sunday morning, Jim Cernero and his wife sat in the audience. I had never seen him direct a choir or lead an audience in worship, yet I felt strongly that God wanted this man to be an integral part of our church. In the middle of the service, I announced, "Jim, I feel this is of the Lord. I believe you are to come and be our music minister."

The entire congregation erupted in spontaneous applause.

God was bringing together quite a team—the Palmquists, Fred Spring, and now Jim Cernero. None of us knew what miracles tomorrow would hold.

STEPPING INTO A NEW ERA

Throughout 1989, every time I prayed I heard the Lord speaking very distinctly about the future. God was clearly directing me: "You will be conducting healing crusades all over the world." Again, just as happened when I gave my heart to the Lord in Toronto many years before, I saw giant stadiums packed to capacity, with people streaming forward to accept Christ.

For some reason, I was reluctant to pray for this to actually take place. I felt so unworthy that God would use me in such a way.

The pages of the calendar continued to turn, yet I avoided praying that prayer. Day after day I would feel the urgency to fall to my knees and ask God to give me a worldwide healing ministry. Yet each time I prayed I could not bring myself to ask God to give me what I knew He had promised.

Finally, the conviction in my heart became overpowering. I went into my study and poured out my heart. "Lord," I cried, "I am giving myself completely to You. I am willing to follow Your direction." At that moment the Lord gave me a vision through which He confirmed His will to me.

The next week, in one of the final services of 1989, I stood before the congregation in Orlando and said, "We are about to step into a new era of ministry—one that will impact our world for eternity! I am filled with expectancy and excitement as I consider ministering in the nineties. Never before have I felt such a stirring in my soul, such anticipation at what is about to break loose on God's people." And I continued, "I have made a decision to be at the forefront of this great revival. I want to be ready to move when God says move, boldly conquering and possessing the land, taking back what Satan has stolen."

GOD'S FORMULA

As 1990 began, I traveled to Singapore to speak at a conference. There, while sitting on the platform, before I was to minister, God began to detail exactly what I was to do when I returned home. Then He said, "Take the message of My saving and healing power to the world through daily television and healing crusades."

Next, the Lord gave me the "formula" of what I was to present on that daily telecast. How blessed I was. He was telling me, "Here's what you do, and here's how you do it."

The Lord instructed, "On the program, pray for the sick, give praise reports, and show My power."

At the same time, God relayed the signal that it was time to schedule major crusades throughout the United States as well as overseas. These were uncharted waters—places I had never gone before.

When people hear that I began preaching in 1974, they assume that from the beginning I had been involved in large meetings with a team of associates. Far from it. With the exception of the weekly services we conducted in Toronto, most of my ministry was at the invitation of a local church or to speak at conferences.

Now, the marching orders God had given were heading me in a totally new direction—to schedule monthly crusades in large auditoriums and arenas.

The minute I returned to Orlando I picked up the phone and called Paul and Jan Crouch, who had become my dear friends. Since 1983 TBN had broadcast our Sunday morning preaching service and the financial arrangement had not changed—TBN gave me the airtime free and we paid all production expenses.

I knew in advance that this request would be different. There would be substantial costs involved, including paying for the airtime. I was also well aware that we didn't have the resources to commit to a daily telecast.

"Paul, this is Benny Hinn," I began, and immediately got right to the point. "I know this is going to be difficult for you to believe, but the Lord told me to call you and ask you to give me a daily half-hour program on TBN."

"Well, it's amazing that you called today," he responded.

"Why?" I wanted to know.

"A program that has been on our network for years is stopping production and you can have the same time slot—11:30 A.M. every morning."

My heart skipped a beat. *Thank You, Lord!* "That is absolutely wonderful," I replied. "Paul, there is only one problem. I don't have the money to pay for the time."

"Benny," he said, "I'm not going to worry about that. You can pay us when the money comes in."

I was walking on clouds. God had not only given me the blueprint, He had gone before me, paving the way.

BOX 90

The first week of March 1990, just days before we were to launch our daily television program, I asked Sheryl Palmquist to go to the Orlando post office. We needed a mailing address that would be easy for our television viewers to remember—hopefully a one- or two-digit number.

"Get the best box number they will give us," I told her. "And be sure it is one we won't have to change."

She returned and said, "Pastor, we can have Box 90."

At that moment, the Lord spoke to my heart and said that would be our address for the nineties—until 1999—after that a change would take place. I only knew the Lord's mandate for that decade.

There was only one dilemma! The post office box was not large; it was the smallest size they offered.

Sheryl talked with the person in charge and said, "We want

to take Box 90, but in the event we receive more mail than this box will physically hold, can we still use the same box?"

"Well, how many letters are you talking about?" he inquired.

Sheryl replied, "Let's say we had one thousand or two thousand pieces of mail in a day. How would you handle that?"

"What makes you think you're going to get that much mail?" he queried.

"Well, you never know," she replied.

The postal officer said, "Lady, if you receive that much mail, you don't have to worry. We will load it in trays and put it in your car when you drive by."

"LOOK AT THIS!"

The first daily broadcast of *This Is Your Day* began on TBN March 5, 1990. At that time the telecast was called *Miracle Invasion.*

The miracle was that we were able to produce the program! We had no studio. Those first broadcasts were taped in my private office, while Sheryl Palmquist, our organist, and Bruce Hughes, our pianist, provided background music from the church platform. Beside me were Dave Palmquist and Kent Mattox.

Kent and his wife began attending our church several years earlier. They had been miraculously saved, and he became the pastor of our singles ministry.

After the program had been airing for a few days, I anxiously asked, "Well, what are the people telling us in the mail? What's the response to the program?"

"We don't know, Pastor," said Dave. "We haven't been down to the post office."

"Well, you'd better get there quick," I told them.

When Dave and Kent retrieved the mail, nearly fifty letters had arrived. "Look at this!" they said, beaming as they opened the envelopes. There were prayer requests, testimonies of healing, people receiving Christ, and some had even sent checks to help defray the cost of the program.

The next day they returned with even more—and what we began to receive was thrilling.

St. Louis, Missouri: "I watch your program every day. I laid my hands on the television screen and I received my healing of a stomach problem."

Port Arthur, Texas: "I was watching your program and the Lord gave you a word of knowledge that there was a woman named Alice that had been praying to be delivered from gluttony. That woman was me. Praise God I am delivered from food addiction."

Salt Lake City, Utah: "I was healed of bursitis and arthritis in my home watching your crusade telecast. I can do things now I haven't been able to do for years. I was using a walker and a wheelchair . . . no more! If it had not been for your TV ministry I don't know what would have happened to me."

Bakersfield, California: "The Lord healed my ulcer while watching your television program. I am new in the Lord and had never watched you before. You were getting ready to pray for the sick. My ulcer had been bothering me. As you prayed you called out 'stomach ulcer' and that was me. I am healed. Thank You, Jesus!"

Evansville, Indiana: "Yesterday, when you asked people to accept Christ as their Savior, I prayed the sinner's prayer with you. I know I will always remember it as the greatest day of my life."

When letters like these began pouring in, I knew God was confirming His mandate. We built a makeshift studio in the overflow room of Orlando Christian Center (later to be called World Outreach Church) and began to add television stations to our network.

Today, we look back and smile, remembering the postal official who scoffed at the idea we would receive perhaps 1,000 or more letters a day. Praise God, we surpassed it.

Now, in an average week we receive anywhere from 20,000 to 30,000 pieces of mail—in addition to thousands of phone calls every day!

CHAPTER 17

JAM BOXES AND BIBLES

The daily telecast was only one part of God's instruction. He also directed me to begin miracle crusades—first in the United States, then into all the world.

In March 1990, the same month the new television program began, we scheduled our first two-day crusade in Phoenix, Arizona, at the four-thousand-seat Valley Cathedral. In the days leading up to the opening service I prayed, "Lord, I'm taking You at Your Word. I am launching out in faith. Please help us to fill this building for Your glory."

When we drove to the auditorium, I could hardly believe it. People were lined up at every door waiting to get in. More than eight thousand showed up that night, and thousands could not enter the building.

After the service I thought, *Well, that was just a one-time phenomenon. Surely it won't happen again tomorrow night!*

The next morning, we began what was to become a permanent feature of our crusades, a morning service with an emphasis on teaching. The service started at 10:00 A.M. By 1:30 in the afternoon I said, "I must stop. It's time for you dear people to go and have your lunch."

One man in the front row yelled out, "You're not quitting! I came a thousand miles for this teaching and you're not quitting!"

The whole audience responded with a shout of agreement. From that first morning session, I knew that people were hungry for the Word of God. At the final service, an even bigger crowd attempted to get into the building.

I told my staff, "It looks like we need to find larger facilities for these meetings."

Within a short period of time our crusades were filling some of the great arenas and coliseums in America—from San Antonio to Charlotte to Long Beach.

HE'S ON THE WAY!

At home, Suzanne was holding down the fort with eight-year-old Jessica and Natasha, who was now six. Of course, I still longed for a baby boy—and I knew what I would call him: *Joshua*.

Years before, Oral Roberts taught me the importance of sowing and reaping. I remember him saying, "When you give your offering, believe for a harvest."

Every Sunday at our church, when the offering plate was passed to me, I would say out loud for everyone to hear, "Thank You, Lord, for my Joshua." It was no secret I wanted a little boy.

In the summer of 1990, on a Sunday evening, just before I walked on the platform, Suzanne came up and placed a pair of little booties on the pulpit. Tied to them was a note that said, "Your Joshua is on the way."

That's how I found out she was pregnant!

Joshua Hinn was born March 23, 1991.

And there was one more surprise in store. The following year, on June 26, 1992, the Lord blessed our home with a beautiful baby girl, Eleasha.

THE TEAM EXPANDS

From the beginning of our crusades, God has surrounded me with an incredible team. Our crusade manager was Charlie McCuen, a talented, hardworking individual who was involved in the visitation ministry of our church. I saw his fervor for God and said, "Lord, You can use that zeal in our crusades." Even though he had never done anything remotely like this before, the Lord used him greatly. Today, Donald Dean, an anointed, gifted gentleman, is doing that same job. Donald, and his wife, Joanne, are a great blessing to me and our work.

Our second crusade was in Anaheim, California, and I invited a singer by the name of Steve Brock to be the guest soloist. I had met him earlier when I was the speaker for a two-day revival sponsored by the Trinity Broadcasting Network.

The first night in Anaheim, I started to sing a chorus, and behind me, Steve began to harmonize. From the moment we started singing that impromptu duet, I felt in my spirit that he should be part of our team.

The following month, I called Alvin Slaughter, a singer who had inspired our people when he came to minister at our church. "Alvin, Steve Brock has just joined our crusade ministry and I feel you also need to be part of what God is doing in these services."

Together, Steve Brock and Alvin Slaughter have touched the lives of millions of people. I am convinced today more than ever that anointed music ushers people into the presence of the Lord.

At a time when I desperately needed administrative help, the Lord sent a man by the name of Gene Polino. He carefully navigated the waters to steer us from our small beginnings to where we are today. Although he no longer works with our ministry, God allowed him to give us direction at this critical time.

In God's perfect timing, Joan Gieson came to work with our crusade healing team for seven years.

Because of the growth of the ministry, the Lord has allowed some outstanding people to be added to our staff, including Tim Lavender, our chief operating officer—he was formerly with the Promise Keepers organization. Also joining us was Peter Ireland, our chief financial officer. These men are wonderful Christians and a great blessing to me and this ministry.

In addition, God has sent to us Michael Ellison of Ellison Media Company in Phoenix, a valued consultant—plus Dennis Brewer and David Middlebrook, Christian attorneys in Dallas, and Jim Guinn, one of the finest CPAs anywhere. These are some of the finest professionals in the business world, who have become my close, dear friends.

Others who have taken roles of leadership include John Wilson, who was a partner with our ministry for many years, Kurt Kjellstrom, who became a very dear friend to my family, Don Boss, who oversees the audio at our crusades, Sue Langford in our follow-up ministry, R. J. Larson, who heads our security team, and Nancy Prichard, who has skillfully handled my personal correspondence and schedule. I thank the Lord daily for these loyal and committed men and women.

The work of Orlando Christian Center—and our crusade outreach—moved steadily forward through the efforts of people such as Mike Thomforde, Steve Hill, Larry Muriello, and Ayub Fleming.

It would be impossible to name all the individuals who, through the years, have enabled our ministry to be what it is today.

Kent Mattox, the young man who joined our church staff in the 1980s, became a source of great strength to me in our crusade ministry. God could not have sent someone more fitting than Kent. He loved life and knew when I needed encouragement. The Lord eventually led Kent into his own ministry, and he will always be my dear friend.

Another person, who was not as high-profile as Kent yet was vital to the early crusade years, was David Delgado from New York City. The son of a Puerto Rican pentecostal preacher, Dave was converted from a life of drug addiction and became a personal assistant to me. His loyalty was unequaled and he was held in great esteem by our staff. Later in his life, after becoming deathly ill with hepatitis, he died prematurely. His death was a mystery to his family, our staff, and myself. Although reports of a drug relapse came to our attention following his death, knowing David as I did—and how deeply he loved God—I can only leave the circumstances of his passing in the hands of the Lord.

For several years in the mid-1990s, Ronn Haus became an associate evangelist on our staff. I had known Ronn for many years—he was the person who introduced me to my future father-in-law, Roy Harthern. Ronn came aboard at a time when I needed a strong spiritual force by my side. He is still close to me in the ministry.

God has also graciously permitted many outstanding ministers of the gospel to become a source of spiritual strength to me— people such as Don George, pastor of Calvary Temple, Dallas,

Texas; Tommy Barnett, pastor of First Assembly of God, Phoenix, Arizona; Jack Hayford, pastor of Church on the Way, Van Nuys, California; Dan Betzer, pastor of First Assembly of God, Ft. Myers, Florida; Ralph Wilkerson, founder and former pastor of Melodyland Christian Center, Anaheim, California; and Fred Roberts, pastor of Durban Christian Center in South Africa.

I have also been greatly influenced by two men who have now gone on to be with the Lord. Soon after my conversion in Toronto I began attending Bibles studies taught by Dr. Winston I. Nunes—one of the great teachers of our generation and a giant in the faith. I still marvel at what I learned from him in my early spiritual walk.

Another man I honor dearly is the late Dr. Lester Sumrall—who left his mark on the church and the world. We continue to work with his sons as they carry the torch of their father's great work.

I am thankful for what these great servants of God have meant to my life.

SPIRITUAL WEALTH

Soon after we began our monthly miracle crusades, I felt led to invite Rex Humbard, the noted evangelist and pioneer of Christian television in America, to be a regular featured speaker for the Friday morning meetings. He is one of the greatest soul winners in the history of evangelism. Rex and his wife, Maude Amiee, were close friends of Kathryn Kuhlman.

Suzanne and I have counted it an honor to spend time with these humble, gracious servants of the Lord. Many times, when I have needed someone to share the burdens of this ministry, Rex has always been there.

I am also grateful to God for sending Oral and Evelyn Roberts into our lives many years ago. The love they have extended to Suzanne and me has been overwhelming.

Only eternity will reveal the spiritual wealth I have received from Oral—and there is not a man on earth that has had a greater impact on my life. I have stated many times, "I love him as my own father."

We also cherish the time we spend with his son and daughter-in-law, Richard and Lindsey.

What a tremendous gift to this world Oral Roberts University has become! He has already left his mark on history. God has used Oral Roberts to lay a mighty foundation for the healing ministry in this world. Millions of lives have been affected by this one man. And the impact of his ministry will be felt for generations to come. The honorary doctorate presented to me at ORU has special meaning because of the man for whom the institution is named.

"THIS IS ALMOST UNREAL"

From the beginning, the impact the miracle crusades were having on cities across the United States was often more than spiritual. For example, when we came to Flint, Michigan, in August 1991, the *Flint Journal* reported in their front-page feature, "They hailed from throughout Michigan, and from Indiana—even Virginia and Tennessee and New Mexico. From all corners of the country they came, descending on Flint's IMA Sports Arena Thursday night, seeking a miracle." The article quoted the spokesperson for the Convention and Tourist Bureau as saying, "Every hotel, motel, and bed-and-breakfast in

Genessee County was booked for Thursday and tonight—
about 2,600 rooms total.

"This is almost unreal," said the spokesperson. "The phones
are ringing off the hook, and I hear it's even worse at the IMA
arena." The news report stated, "Some crusade enthusiasts
camped outside the arena Wednesday night so they could be
first in line for the free first-come, first-served seats. Others came
early Thursday morning, packing blankets and lawn chairs,
coolers, jam boxes, and their Bibles."

Similar reports began to follow the crusades across America.

MIRACLES IN THE RAIN

God's mandate to me also included taking the gospel to the
nations of the world—and not just a token visit to a foreign
city. We prepared for major crusades in these countries as we
did in the United States, involving scores of local churches and
missionaries, a crusade choir, altar workers, and a follow-up
program for new converts.

At the crusade in Manila in the Philippines, in February 1992,
the Araneta Coliseum was filled—with thousands more standing
outside. The news reported that many arrived as early as four
o'clock in the morning just to wait for the evening service.

When we returned to the Philippines sometime later,
500,000 people attended the first night of the meeting.

Often, our overseas journeys are accompanied by the unexpected. At our 1994 crusade at Huracan Stadium in Buenos
Aires, Argentina, as the crowds gathered early in the day, rain
began to fall—and the deluge continued all afternoon. The

stadium officials refused to allow the meeting to take place that evening due to the potential safety risk from uncovered electrical wires on the soccer field.

That night, God worked in an unusual way. We were given time on a major commercial network to conduct a live miracle service on national television. The broadcast reached most of Argentina, plus parts of three adjoining South American countries. Miracles took place in the studio audience and reports of healing began flooding in from viewers.

The next night the 100,000-seat Huracan Stadium was literally overflowing. Thousands stood on the muddy, rain-soaked field praising and worshiping the Lord as the choir sang, "Nada Es Impossible" (Nothing Is Impossible). The following morning nine thousand pastors packed a downtown arena as I preached on "No Retirement in the Kingdom."

To this day we hear reports of churches that are still experiencing revival because of the spiritual outpouring pastors received from the Lord in that meeting. To Jesus belongs all the glory.

A FRAGRANCE, A WIND

In crusades in the United States and overseas, I never cease to be amazed at the demonstration of God's power.

One night, at a service in Detroit, the presence of the Lord was so awesome that you could smell its fragrance—a fragrance that permeated the building so that thousands testified to experiencing it. I am convinced that the presence of God intensifies when there is total unity of believers in the service.

In Pretoria, South Africa, a wind was felt by thousands that started in the upper part of the building and swept across the entire audience.

In Bogatá, Colombia, the presence of the Holy Spirit was so awesome that the Lord spoke to me and said, "In one hour I am going to walk in here." I looked at my watch and it was ten minutes until eight o'clock.

Immediately, I paused to tell the crowd exactly what the Lord had just said. Then we continued with the service. One hour later, at ten minutes to nine, the power and presence of God hit the building with such magnitude that people in that circular building began falling from the outside in—all in the same direction—as if a giant wave had hit them. If you can imagine a circle, then another circle within it, and a smaller circle in the middle. When the power of God hit, people fell in perfect waves around those circles until practically every person in that building was on the floor.

It was a time of great emotion and people were quite shaken by the experience. I had never witnessed anything like it before.

In that same service, about thirty minutes later, the Lord stopped me again and instructed me to have the people become quiet. He said, "Tell them as they listen, they will hear the singing of angels."

That is exactly what took place.

HUNGRY FOR THE ANOINTING

People have asked me, "Benny, why do you think your crusade ministry burst onto the world scene with such force at the start of the 1990s?"

I can list several reasons. I feel that people began attending our meetings in great numbers because they were hungry for the anointing of God—and they wanted to be in an atmosphere where it is present.

In these crusades it is not uncommon to see hundreds of ministers at the morning service, weeping, deeply moved, seeking the anointing of the Holy Spirit.

The television program certainly contributed to the large crusades since every day people all over the world were able to see the power of God displayed.

In 1990, a book I was inspired to write, *Good Morning, Holy Spirit,* was released by Thomas Nelson Publishers. To the surprise of everyone involved in the project—including me—the book began flying off the bookshelves. Stores could not keep them in stock, and it zoomed to the top of the Christian bookseller charts. It remained there for sixteen months.

Millions of copies were sold in the United States and through more than forty foreign translations. *Christianity Today* reported that it is "one of the best-selling Christian books of all time."

The president and CEO of Thomas Nelson Publishers, Sam Moore, and his brother Chuck Moore, two gentlemen of Lebanese origin, have become my dear friends. Over the years they have been great supporters of this ministry.

TWISTING SCRIPTURE?

If *Good Morning, Holy Spirit* had met with mediocre success, no one would have paid much attention. However, because of its rocketlike rise in Christian publishing, the critics had a heyday.

They swooped down on the manuscript like vultures—trying to find something to pick apart.

One organization in particular, the Christian Research Institute (CRI), in Irvine, California, took great exception to many of the teachings in the book. To most observers, however, the underlying problem was whether a person believed that spiritual gifts are available for Christians today.

I had no problem revising some passages of the book for clarification; however, I was not about to change my belief about the work of the Holy Spirit.

Hank Hanegraff, president of CRI, charged me with "twisting Scripture."

When he began to bring my name up on his radio program, I felt it was important for me to meet with him and talk about some of the issues he had discussed. We met on several occasions.

I do admit there have been times when I have made a statement that was incorrect. Because we are continually growing in the Lord, preachers and laypeople alike must be open to the Lord's correction. However, I do not believe it is right when a minister corrects his theology—or his view on a point of Scripture—and the critics continue to bring up that same subject.

"LET'S NOT BE FOOLISH"

Since we are a high-profile ministry, I've come to expect scrutiny from the media— and we certainly have had our share. We have been the focus of national television investigative reports. In every case, these reports have helped the ministry to become stronger.

The Lord has also opened doors allowing me to appear on

programs such as *Larry King Live,* where I have been warmly received. I have found many in the secular media to be fair in their coverage of our ministry. I told one reporter, "I have far more difficulty with religious extremists who believe they are God's messengers."

How can I criticize the press when they have attracted hundreds of thousands of people to our crusades to hear the Word? Many of these people have been wonderfully saved and miraculously healed. Thank God, all things work together for good.

CHAPTER 18

THE CRUSADE EXPERIENCE

Some people see a marquee on an arena that reads, "Benny Hinn Miracle Crusade" and mistakenly think that I have some kind of special healing power. Far from it. What happens in our meetings has absolutely nothing to do with me—*it has everything to do with the fact that the healing power of the Holy Spirit is available to all.*

It is the working of the Spirit that brings healing, deliverance, and salvation.

How do I prepare myself to become an instrument of the Lord? Those who know our ministry—especially members of our crusade team—fully understand that I have to literally separate myself from the world before I walk on that platform.

Our typical crusade includes three services: Thursday night, Friday morning, and Friday night. Starting at two o'clock on Thursday afternoon, everything about my life changes. My immediate staff knows there are to be no phone calls from my office and no interruptions of any kind. That is when I begin to prepare myself physically, mentally, and spiritually for the first service. I ask God to help me become ready in every way. I don't want to be lacking in any area—especially spiritually.

God cannot use a heart that is distracted and a body that is exhausted. I've got to be a vessel He can use. That's why I will not allow anyone to disturb me—regardless of who they are. Perhaps more than any other people, my wife and children fully understand and appreciate how I feel about becoming ready for a miracle service.

Friday is the same. No disruptions. I won't permit anything to pollute my mind, body, or spirit. No radio or television. No newspaper. No outside influences.

Why is this so vital? I am fully aware of the fact that thousands of people have made great sacrifices, and often have traveled long distances, to attend these meetings. Many are suffering with incurable diseases and infirmities, praying that this will be their moment of healing. Can I do any less than to totally prepare myself and surrender to the Lord?

I learned many years ago that the only way I could have a successful ministry was to find people who are just as anointed in their ministries as I am in mine. Then I have to trust them to run their offices so I can be free to focus on ministry. If they can't be trusted, then it is time for them to move on.

A SENSE OF EXPECTANCY

Anyone arriving early for one of our crusades will sense the faith and expectation. Often it is drizzling and still dark when people begin to line up for a meeting that will not begin for another twelve or fourteen hours. These people are hungry for God and willing to wait for the best seats.

Some come with bags full of snacks, books, and other items to help pass the time. They spend the day making friends with others in line—talking, reading, singing, praying, and waiting for the time the doors will open.

By midday the lines will have lengthened considerably, and most people know what those around them have come expecting—they are expecting miracles.

Inside, about seventy-five key volunteers (from a master list of about two hundred regulars) are at their posts. These are professional people from all over the country who, at their own expense, are at our monthly crusades. The regular volunteers coordinate the activities of hundreds of local people who come to help—from an army of ushers to those who will assist the healing team.

When the doors finally open and the people rush toward their seats, the chatter of voices creates an excited roar throughout the building. The crusade choir is already in place, and as they begin to rehearse, many onlookers sing along. The atmosphere seems charged, and an anointing of God's presence has already begun to descend.

On the main level, ministry team workers are encouraging the sick and sharing testimonies of healing. As the choir continues to rehearse, the seats are filling fast. Volunteer workers rush here and there all over the arena, finalizing everything in preparation for the service.

At 7:00 P.M. the lights dim, and the roar of voices becomes a hushed silence as an announcer's voice welcomes the thousands who have gathered for the miracle service. Blue lights slowly embrace the silhouette of Bruce Hughes seated at a 9-foot Steinway piano, playing a favorite old hymn with artistic perfection. A final arpeggio on the keyboard signals the end of the solo.

Resounding applause welcomes Jim Cernero, our music director, as he takes his place before the one-thousand-voice crusade choir. As they sing, the momentum builds and soon people stand all over the arena as the mass choir begins, "Then sings my soul, My Savior, God, to Thee: / How great Thou art! How great Thou art!"

The thousands who fill the arena are lifted into a place of glorious praise and worship.

I cannot begin to describe what I am feeling as I walk onto the platform at that moment and continue to lead the audience in worship. Everything I have prayed for—everything God has prepared my life for—seems wrapped up in that moment. And I know that the Holy Spirit is about to descend with great power!

Steve Brock and other special soloists sing crusade favorites, and the love of God becomes almost tangible. Many faces are streaked with tears as people from many different backgrounds bask in God's presence. The expressions on their faces tell any observer that Jesus Christ is real, He loves them, and He is present to touch them and meet their needs.

As I begin to preach the Word of God, faith rises.

At one point in the service I give an altar call: "If you want to give your heart to Jesus Christ, if you want to know Him as your Savior and Lord, come down to the front of the platform where I can pray with you." I stand in awe every time I see the people streaming to the front, filling every aisle. As the choir sings "Just As I Am," thousands give their lives to Jesus Christ. Later, as they walk back to their seats, I often lead a beautiful song of worship and the crowd joins in.

"THANK YOU FOR YOUR MERCY!"

The time passes quickly and worship fills the arena once more. What seemed impossible for some just hours earlier, is now possible. The God of miracles is here.

Often I will become suddenly filled with a fiery presence that envelops me, and I begin to pray with authority, rebuking sickness and disease. "If God has touched you, line up to my left and my right," I request. Many are already there, anxious to testify of God's healing power in their life.

At the side of the platform a member of our healing team reports, "Pastor, this lady has come all the way from Cincinnati, Ohio, believing for God to heal her from cancer. She has no more pain!"

At that moment all I can say is "Dear Jesus, thank You for Your mercy." The audience erupts in applause and praise in gratitude for what God has done.

People come, one after another, to declare they have been healed by the power of God. Cancer, asthma, heart disease, diabetes, emphysema, alcoholism, drug addiction, and more.

The power of God often explodes in the arena—and in every heart—as onlookers rejoice with each person who steps onto the platform to tell of God's divine touch upon them.

When the last song has been sung and the crowd begins to disperse and file out of the auditorium, I seldom want to leave the platform. Faces are radiant, beaming, full of life and joy. It is apparent they have experienced the presence of God in a way they never imagined possible. I pray that because of that experience, they will never be the same again.

CRUSADER 1

If you walk behind the crusade stage, past a corridor of black curtains, you'll find Crusader 1—our state-of-the-art mobile television production unit. This forty-nine-foot custom-built truck trailer contains the highest-quality equipment for capturing on video every detail of what you see on *This Is Your Day!*

Jeff Pittman, our television producer, is one of the finest in the industry. Even more, he feels divinely called to stand by my side in spreading the message of the gospel. We have spent hundreds of hours together in all parts of the world and I know the dedication with which he approaches his task. Jeff's goal is to capture the anointing in the services and minister to a person's need—whether it's a Christian who is discouraged, an alcoholic who needs deliverance, a mother whose son just ran away from home, or a husband whose wife just took the children and left.

Working closely with him are directors Truett Hancock and Gene Bailey—and the longtime announcer for the program, Keith Curtis.

Jeff and I talk about every facet of the program, from a particular song we will use to the testimony of someone who has been healed. And before every broadcast we pray that viewers will be touched by God's power.

Every time I receive a letter telling me "I was saved by watching the program," or "I was healed through your television ministry," I know it was not by accident. To our television crew, their work is a ministry.

We recently dedicated our new World Media Center studio in Aliso Viejo, California. Our equipment rivals that of any network studio in Los Angeles or New York—and it's all for the glory of God.

I am convinced that we must "speak peace to the nations . . . to the ends of the earth" (Zech. 9:10). My goal is to somehow reach every home in every country with the gospel. We are taking the message of God's saving and healing power into every nation that will accept our broadcast.

Many governments that have long forbidden the Christian message are now being reached via satellite.

This unique television outreach is part of God's calling on my life.

THE MISSION OF MAX

Parked outside every crusade arena you'll see dozens of buses—church buses, school buses, charters and tour buses. For many people, this is a ministry in itself.

Max Colver, of Indianapolis, became involved in bringing people to our crusades when he assisted his aging mother in leaving a crowded Chicago arena after a Miracle Crusade in 1992. As they watched people climb aboard, Max realized that those who came on buses were assured a seat earlier than the general public. It was the beginning of a unique ministry.

The first trip he organized was to our crusade in Cincinnati a few months later. And now he has accompanied more than 1,200 people to twelve more crusades. In addition, Max began a church in Indianapolis called Living Word. He says, "It was birthed out of the anointing we received in the meetings."

Pastor Colver and his wife focus on taking the burden of travel off the shoulders of the elderly and sick, providing safety and comfort throughout the entire crusade experience.

They begin planning for the trip two or three months before one of our crusades. Then he rents the buses and the hotel rooms and charges about $100 for the package.

What's important to Max are results. He told us that many

bus travelers come expecting miracles. "A lot of handicapped people are on the trip, and many of our people get healed," he said. "The long bus ride allows an atmosphere of faith to be created. We stay focused," said Pastor Max. "The first thing I say every morning is, 'Praise God! This is your day for a miracle!'"

They even watch a video of one of our services on the journey. And many miracles actually take place during the bus trips to and from the miracle services. "We were driving to Nashville, and halfway there I heard a shout in the back of the bus. Someone was healed," said Max. "As we travel back to Indianapolis, we let people give their testimonies. And some are healed on the way home. It's glorious," he says.

PHYSICIANS IN MINISTRY

When we began our church in Orlando, among our first members were Donald Colbert, M.D., and his wife, Mary. Don is a Spirit-filled family doctor in Longwood, Florida, who is my personal physician and also assists us in the crusades.

We have physicians at our meetings to check those who claim to have been healed during the services. Their work is very important to us. Because of their medical training, crusade physicians are able to conduct a cursory examination of those who have been touched by God's power. They help confirm a person's healing before sending him or her up to the platform to give a testimony.

Why would medical physicians volunteer to take part in a Miracle Crusade? In this case they share a unique perspective of the miraculous healing power of Jesus.

Dr. Sydel Barnes, another of our crusade physicians, has her practice in the inner city of Tampa, Florida. Several years ago she attended one of our crusades in Atlanta, and said, "As a physician, it was an experience that surpassed anything I thought I would ever see." She added, "I remember in particular a little boy with cerebral palsy. I was sitting high in the rafters somewhere, and I was looking down at him. As someone prayed for the child, I saw the Spirit of God come upon him. He began to run, when he was previously unable to walk," she said. "I knew this was something far beyond medical knowledge and rationalization."

Dr. Barnes was overcome by what she witnessed in that meeting. She began to pray, "Lord, I want to be like one of the disciples who walked with Jesus. I want to be part of these miracles."

She allots the time in her busy schedule to volunteer at most of our crusades.

Dr. Daniel Gorduek began helping at our meetings after he was miraculously healed of cancer in one of our crusades in Puerto Rico. In 1996 he was diagnosed with prostate cancer of an aggressive type that had spread to his bones. He was given no hope for survival. Today he is cancer-free and volunteers his time as a crusade physician.

Volunteers—televisions crews—bus ministries—crusade physicians—they are all crucial members of a team that is dedicated to reaching the world for Christ.

CHAPTER 19

THE GREATEST GIFT

It was late in the evening and I was relaxing, seated in a comfortable chair with my son, Joshua, sprawled on my lap. That same afternoon I had flown in from a crusade on the West Coast, and my boy, who was about five at the time, was so excited to see his daddy.

Down the hallway, I could hear the familiar busy sounds of Jessica and Natasha getting ready for bed. Eleasha, our youngest daughter, was already sleeping.

As the house grew quiet, Joshua snuggled closer to me. When I glanced down I noticed that he was fast asleep in my arms. He looked so peaceful nestled there—almost angelic. I sat quietly, stroking his brown hair, cherishing the moment. I thought, *What a wonderful gift from the Lord.*

God has allowed me to traverse the world, meet distinguished leaders of many nations, and do many things, yet these experiences pale in comparison to the precious moments I spend with my children. As a father, there is nothing I would not do for my Jessica, Natasha, Joshua, and Eleasha. I love them.

Each of my children is special, and God has made them unique individuals.

JESSICA

Our oldest daughter, Jessica, has grown to be a tall, lovely, confident young lady. Sometimes I tease her about looking just like me, and she quickly responds with a twinkle in her dark eyes, "Remember, I'm English, too, like Mom!"

Certainly, there is a degree of pressure on our children because of the high-profile nature of our ministry, yet it doesn't seem to unduly bother them. When Jessica was a sophomore at Lake Mary High School, she was the focus of a feature article in the *Orlando Sentinel.* She told the reporter, "To me it's not like living with someone famous. It's just my dad." And she added, "My dad and I are very close. We are exactly alike."

When Jessica turned sixteen I gave her a cell phone. There was a reason for my gift. As she told a friend, "It's amazing. No matter where my dad may be in the world, he always knows what time my curfew is and I know that phone is going to ring. Sure enough, it's Dad."

Thank God for modern technology!

Suzanne and I have been thrilled to see Jessica's strength of character and her great compassion toward others.

NATASHA

Our second daughter, Natasha, fills our house with life and excitement—she is always bubbling. By choice, she doesn't seek attention publicly, saying as little as possible. Privately, however, she doesn't hold much back! The minute I walk into the house I can always count on her to give me an opinion and tell me exactly what's on her mind.

"Tasha" as we call her, is extremely self-disciplined. She's the one who comes home from school and tackles her homework immediately—totally finishing her assignments before any leisure activities.

Since early childhood, Natasha has had a passion for missions, and talked about children she wanted to help in foreign lands. She jumped at the opportunity to travel to Zambia and Mexico—not to attend our crusades, but to work and minister with other young people on trips organized by the church my brother Sammy pastors in Orlando.

JOSHUA

Joshua? Well, he's all boy. Just mention any sport and he's ready to tackle it—basketball, soccer, karate, and especially hockey. I was amazed the first time I saw him speed down the floor of a gym playing hockey on Rollerblades.

My Joshua is always full of surprises and I'm never quite sure what to expect. He's definitely not shy when I invite him to join me on the platform. Since he was three or four he would jump at the chance to grab the microphone and say "Hello" or ask to sing a song. The "Hello" is by far the most predictable. I remember bringing him to the platform at a December crusade and he wanted to sing a Christmas song. "What would you like to sing?" I asked him.

"Dashing Through the Snow," he replied.

Since this was a Miracle Crusade, I had hoped he would at least choose, "Silent Night" or "Away in a Manger." No. He wanted to sing "Dashing Through the Snow," so that's exactly what the people heard that night!

My heart is filled with expectation for Joshua's future.

ELEASHA

Our youngest daughter is Eleasha, the "baby" of the family, yet she is growing by leaps and bounds. What a sweetheart she is—such a peaceful child and a joy to be near. My wife, Suzanne, and I can hardly remember a time when she has cried for any reason. Regardless of the circumstances, we can count on Eleasha to be happy.

Even from early infancy, when it was time for bed, she would lie down, close her eyes, and go to sleep. No protest, no tears, no delay, just, "Night, night."

She's just as content playing alone or with other children—it seems to make little difference. Many nights, I'll look and find her in her room, engrossed in a book or drawing a picture.

Eleasha is equally at home taking ballet lessons, joining a karate class, or singing on the platform with her brother, Joshua. She loves everything—especially her brother. They are inseparable.

HUGS, KISSES, AND CARDS

Someone asked me recently, "What is the best Christmas present you ever received from your kids?"

I didn't have to think long for the answer. Every Christmas and on our birthdays, Suzanne and I receive a special card from each of our children. The message is not something they have purchased in a store, but words they have written from their hearts. More than once I have wiped a tear from my eye when I read, "Merry Christmas to the greatest daddy in the whole wide world," or "I love you on your birthday, and every day of the year."

Hugs, kisses, and cards—these are the presents I will always treasure.

Some people are surprised when they first spend time around our children. One minister friend commented, "I'm shocked. They're all so *normal*—so down to earth."

I laughed and replied, "Isn't that how they're supposed to be?"

They are typical, active kids, each with a unique temperament. Joshua and Jessica are more strong-willed and assertive, while Natasha and Eleasha have personalities that are tranquil and passive. We thank God they are all such loving children.

DECISIONS, DECISIONS

Suzanne and I made a decision early in our marriage that when we became parents we would give our children the love, security, and discipline they needed, yet we would not isolate them from the real world. For example, in the lower grades our children have gone to private Christian schools. In high school, however, Jessica and Natasha have attended public schools—and their faith and Christian commitment have remained strong. We have been especially pleased with the acceptance our children have received in public schools.

Oh, there have been times when other kids have taunted them—for example, making fun of people falling under the power of God. It's interesting to note, however, that such things happened in a Christian institution, not in a public school.

Our kids are not perfect. As young people they have experienced typical adolescent struggles, but God has been faithful, and we are so proud of the way they conduct their lives.

As parents, we have tried to give our children guidelines and let them be kids; to learn from their mistakes and to do their own growing up. Suzanne was raised as a PK—a "preacher's kid"—and her mother told her, "I don't expect you to be the best kid in the church, but please don't be the worst." We have raised our children with the same philosophy.

One of the great quandaries I have faced is trying to obey the call of God on my life for a worldwide ministry and be a responsible husband and father.

There have been many sleepless nights when Suzanne has felt as though she were raising the children alone—and at times has almost collapsed under the burden. More than once she has stood on the promise of the Word that God "would be a husband to me and a father to my children." The Lord has never, never failed.

Earlier, I spoke of the time when Suzanne and I were first married and she traveled with me to all of our meetings. She is a woman of prayer and obeys the voice of the Lord.

When Jessica was born, Suzanne said, "Benny, I know you want me with you in the meetings, but I feel that God needs me here—at home—giving Jessica all of my attention." She took it as a calling. Then came Natasha, Joshua, and Eleasha, and she has never wavered in her conviction to be a strong anchor for our family. I thank God every day for His cover of blessing on Suzanne and on our home.

Now, with our oldest children becoming young adults, Suzanne is becoming more involved in our public ministry, yet she still believes our children and myself are her number one priority. As she often comments, "Ministry begins in the home."

IT HAPPENED AT THE POND

I could never begin to count the hours we have spent on our knees praying for each of our children.

"Lord, I give You Jessica," I would pray. "Protect her from harm. May she always love You."

"And now Natasha, Lord. Hold her in Your loving arms, and never let her go."

Then I would pray for Joshua, "God, may he become a man of righteousness—and a strong warrior for You."

"And Eleasha, Lord. I give this beautiful child to Your care. Never let her stray from You."

In the years that have so quickly passed, I have stood on the platforms of the world and prayed the prayer of faith for millions of people. From Singapore to South Africa, entire families have received God's anointing and been touched by His power. But what about my own family? What about my children? I prayed that they, too, would experience the reality of the Holy Spirit. At an early age, they had asked the Lord to come into their hearts, but I wanted them to experience everything God had for them.

On October 8, 1998, we were holding a miracle service at an arena known as "The Pond," in Anaheim, California. I had conducted meetings in southern California many times, yet that night the Spirit of God was like a fire—people could feel the anointing spreading all over the building.

I looked down on the front row and there were Suzanne and our four beautiful children, who had flown in from Orlando to be with me. As people were worshiping in the Spirit, I was praying, "Lord, touch my children tonight. May they know Your mighty power."

It was during this time that Jessica, who had just begun her junior year of high school, had been going through typical adolescent adjustments, and as parents we were concerned.

That night I felt led to ask my children to come to the platform—I was going to introduce them to the audience. However, God had something else in mind. The moment they approached me in the center of the stage, the anointing became so strong that when I turned toward them, all four of my children fell to the floor. There were Jessica, Natasha, Joshua, and Eleasha, slain in the Spirit by the power of God. It was a beautiful sight, and I began to weep before the Lord. When something like that happens to your own children, it is an incredible feeling.

God did an amazing work that night. When they returned to Orlando their Christian witness took on a boldness we had never seen—and the effects of that meeting are still evident.

The story of my children remains to be written. I can only pray that each chapter will be filled with faith, hope, and love.

CHAPTER 20

A MIRACULOUS
PROPHECY FULFILLED

In the late 1970s, I spoke in Dallas, Texas, at the ministerial training institute, Christ for the Nations. I left the platform with the director of the ministry, Mrs. Frieda Lindsay, a wonderful friend and the wife of the founder of CFN, the late Gordon Lindsay. Beside me, I noticed that a gentleman with white hair was following us.

"Young man! Young man!" he said, in a strong, forceful voice.

As I looked back, the man began to prophesy. "Thus saith the Lord," he began. "The day will come when you will preach My gospel in the Arab world."

I looked at Mrs. Lindsay and quietly commented, "This man is crazy!"

She did not respond, and I continued, "There is no way I would be permitted to go and preach in the Arab world—even if I wanted to. My passport says 'Born in Israel.'"

Mrs. Lindsay turned to me, and with a knowing look on her face, said, "This man has never been wrong." And she dismissed the incident.

MISSING THE PLANE

A short time later I was at the airport in Ottawa, Canada, with Harald Bredesen, who was about to catch a plane to another city. Bredesen is one of God's choice servants—a former Lutheran minister who invented the term "charismatic renewal."

We were in the airport restaurant and the waitress had just taken our order. I asked Harald, "What time does your plane leave?" He looked at his watch and realized the flight was leaving in ten minutes. We grabbed his two large suitcases and headed straight for the gate—only to be told, "You'll have to go to the main counter to check those in."

With that mission accomplished, Harald ran for his plane. About halfway up the stairs, he paused, turned around and announced, "But Benny, I'm not finished talking with you." Then he calmly walked back down to the tarmac.

He sauntered into the terminal—as if he had all the time in the world. Harald then placed his hands on my shoulders and began to talk. "Benny, God has given me a word for you."

"I'm ready to receive it," I answered with curiosity.

"God has told me that He is going to use you to reach the Arab world—beginning with the heads of state." And he added, "You are going to be preaching all over the Middle East."

I looked out the window just in time to see Harald's plane taking off—with his luggage on board. It didn't seem to faze him at all. "Oh, don't worry," he said and smiled. "I'll catch the next flight. I just felt you needed to hear this."

Only a few months later, on March 27, 1979, the headline of the *Jerusalem Post* read, "Israel and Egypt Sign Peace Treaty

Declaring End to 30-Year State of War." It was Israel's first-ever peace treaty with a neighboring Arab state and a fulfillment of Isaiah 19.

IT'S IN MY BLOOD

Many times I have been asked, "Benny, what are your dreams? What are your goals? If there was something you could accomplish that would have special significance, what would it be?"

Since my call to ministry I have had a burning desire to bring the message of Jesus Christ and the power of the Holy Spirit to my homeland—and to the nations of the Middle East. Although I have strayed far from its shores, I can still feel the sand of the Mediterranean under my feet. Jaffa is still in my blood, and every week I take time to read the international edition of the *Jerusalem Post.*

In several unique ways, the prophecy spoken by the gentleman in Dallas and Harald Bredesen began to unfold.

Through the Voice of Hope—a television station founded by George Otis in Lebanon, and now owned and operated by CBN—and through satellite, our ministry has developed a large and loyal audience in Israel and several surrounding Arab nations. We receive letters from viewers in Syria, Jordan, and Egypt saying, "My life has been transformed."

Travelers staying in the hotels of Jerusalem watch *This Is Your Day* on cable television—and it is seen in homes all over the nation. As a result, when I have meetings in Israel, thousands come to see the power of God.

I believe it is providential that I was born in the land of the

Bible. In both the Jewish and Arab worlds we are received by people and many governments with open arms.

I love it when people in the region see my olive complexion and tell me, "You look like one of us." I'm proud of that fact.

A ROYAL INVITATION

In 1997, before his death, I had the honor of meeting privately with His Majesty, King Hussein of Jordan. Our conversation focused on the process and prospects for peace in the Middle East and on the passion of his heart—the care and welfare of children in his country. Later, we would see firsthand the commitment King Hussein made to the orphans of his nation.

Both the king and his firstborn son, Prince Abdullah (who has now succeeded him as king), greeted our television audience and extended a personal invitation for us to visit Jordan.

For two decades we had taken thousands of partners and friends with us to Israel—filling as many as six 747's in one trip. And now we were being invited to bring a large group to Jordan.

The minister of tourism for that nation came to our Nashville, Tennessee, crusade and addressed our audience with a message on the importance of Arabs and Jews learning to live together harmoniously.

EVENTFUL DAYS IN AMMAN

Amman, Jordan, is quite a contrast from the lush green foliage and often muggy weather of Orlando, Florida. From my hotel window, I was drinking in the brilliant blue sky—not a cloud in sight. The air was desert dry. The days were hot—and the nights brought little relief. Low white-stucco buildings stretched off toward the gently rolling hills in the distance. The predominant color was brown—in all different hues—interrupted occasionally by the dusty greens of scrubby vegetation.

The invitation of King Hussein to come to his nation and the permission to minister freely was now a reality. It was September 1998.

More than two thousand of our partners had traveled with us by plane to Israel, and most extended the journey to include these eventful days in Jordan. This is the land on which Moses, Elijah, Elisha, and so many biblical figures walked. We were taken by government guides to Mount Nebo, the location from which God showed Moses the promised land, just before his death, and to the recently discovered site from where Elijah ascended to heaven. We also visited Aaron's tomb near historic Petra.

We were escorted to a former residence of King Hussein—a beautiful palace that he designated to become an orphanage. Until his death, the king was in contact, almost daily, with these needy children. He knew them by name and was concerned for their future.

In Amman, we met with Princess Rania (now Queen of Jordan) to present the nation's needy with 1,200 cases of medical and surgical supplies and 45,000 pounds of assorted dry goods—including flour, beans, and potatoes. The food distribution was a combined effort between our ministry and LeSea, the continuing work of the late Dr. Lester Sumrall.

Princess Rania coordinated the effort through the royal family, and personally assisted us in distributing food to many underprivileged Jordanians.

THE HEM OF HIS GARMENT

"We have arranged for you to use the Palace of Culture," a government official informed me. The four-thousand-seat building is the largest auditorium in Amman—an impressive meeting place reserved for special events and invited guests. Now it was being made open to the public for our meeting. I was told that the significance of this invitation could not be overstated.

It was incredible. As a child in Jaffa I never believed for a second that I would step into an Arab country. And now I was standing in the capital of Jordan, preaching as not only the guest of the government, but protected by national soldiers. Amazing!

The building was filled to capacity, and officials of His Majesty were there to welcome our crusade team to the country. Because of our television outreach in the area, people came from several Arab countries—Lebanon, Egypt, Syria, and Iraq.

I can still speak enough Arabic to communicate, but for this service we used an interpreter so I could be free to minister as I have around the world. My message that night was about the woman who touched the hem of Jesus' garment, and I told the people, "If you reach out and touch Him, you can also be saved and healed."

On faces across that auditorium I could see a hunger for the Word of God. Then, when we led people in praise and worship, miracles began to take place and people testified to what God was doing.

I didn't alter my message simply because I was in another culture. Without hesitation, I invited people to ask Christ into their hearts—to become their personal Savior. From all parts of that building they came streaming to the front. I could hardly believe what I was seeing. I thought to myself, *Am I really preaching the gospel in an Arab country? Is this really happening?*

I asked the people to repeat after me in Arabic. "Lord Jesus, I'm a sinner. Forgive my sin. Come into my heart. I give You my life. I surrender all. Wash me in Your blood. Make me clean, dear Jesus. Fill me with Your Spirit. Come and touch my life right now. Amen."

The Lord had allowed me to return to this war-ravaged land and walk through doors that only He could open.

God's timetable for the Middle East is still unfolding. From the invitations we continue to receive from government leaders in the region, I believe entire nations are going to meet the Prince of Peace.

As I write this book, the Lord has already opened the doors for me to minister in eight Arab nations.

The journey has only begun.

CHAPTER 21

A Transforming Touch

In 1972, almost simultaneously with my conversion, God told me I was to preach the gospel and bring people to the cross of His dear Son—that was my primary responsibility.

Now, after twenty-five years of ministry, I am placing more attention on soul winning than ever. Although I have always focused on the message of salvation, the Lord has impressed upon me the need for an even greater emphasis. The most incredible harvest of souls we have ever seen occurred when we took our team to Trinidad, Jamaica, New Guinea, Hungary, the Ukraine, and Guyana.

We traveled to Papua New Guinea, at the official invitation of the prime minister, Bill Skate, who personally requested that I come and speak to the nation. What a glorious time it was! In excess of 300,000 people attended the services daily. I was invited to speak at a special prayer breakfast with the Parliament and to pray for the nation's leadership. The front page of the national newspaper featured the crusade under the banner "The Power of Faith."

It's impossible to describe how I felt when Prime Minister Skate stood before the vast audience and declared, "The prime minister of this country is none other than Jesus Christ!"

Most important, *an entire nation was touched by the mighty power of the Holy Spirit.* I am still praising God.

A few weeks later, in Jamaica, more than 200,000 attended one service—government officials told us it was the largest crowd ever gathered together in the history of the nation. Next, in Kiev in the Ukraine, when I gave the invitation for souls, people came flooding to the front from all over that packed soccer stadium—including some who had watched the entire service perched in the branches of trees. They were like Zacchaeus of old, who came down from a sycamore tree in Jericho to meet Jesus.

I praised God and said, "Thank You, Lord, for the greatest outpouring in these twenty-five years of ministry."

In just these few international crusades upward of 350,000 people publicly accepted Christ as their Savior—and even more through our daily television program, *This Is Your Day,* and United States crusades. And again, to our wonderful Lord Jesus, belongs all the glory.

BY ALL MEANS

On December 4, 1998, surrounded by pioneers of Christian television and noted ministers from around the world, we dedicated our new World Media Center, in Aliso Viejo, California. From this state-of-the-art studio and production facility we are able to expand our global television outreach.

Why am I so committed to reaching the lost through every means possible? Jesus said, "This gospel of the kingdom will be preached in all the world as a witness to all the nations, and then the end will come" (Matt. 24:14).

In addition to television and the printed word, our partners around the world have enabled us to touch the lives of the needy—including helping thousands of orphans on a continuing basis.

I thank the Lord for our partners daily. Without them, these things would not be possible—and I know one day the Lord Himself will reward each of them. These dear people have sacrificially given—and continue to give—to see souls saved, bodies healed, and multitudes delivered from the power of the enemy.

When I began this ministry, after the great visitation I received from the Lord, I wondered how God would accomplish the vision. Now I know. He is doing it through His wonderful people. And to every partner reading this book, I say from the bottom of my heart, "Thank you! Thank you! Thank you!"

A NEW ERA

Earlier I explained the significance of Box 90 in Orlando. At the time, God spoke to my heart and said that would be our address for the nineties—until 1999—but after that a change would take place.

During the decade God blessed our ministry beyond measure and our headquarters in Orlando was bursting at the seams. Workers were scattered across the complex. And after looking at the situation it was clear we had outgrown the property.

We were faced with the prospect of outsourcing parts of our ministry and moving people to other facilities. I knew that remaining in our present location would stifle and perhaps even halt our growth. "Lord, are You talking to me?" I questioned.

Throughout the years God has directed me with lights that were either red or green—never yellow. His leading has always been clear.

Three years earlier my wife, Suzanne, startled me when she said, "Benny, the Lord spoke to me and said that the headquarters of the healing ministry would move to Dallas, Texas."

"Dallas?" I responded in amazement. "Well, if God is really talking to you, please tell the Lord to also speak to me." And the subject was dropped.

One year later, something quite similar happened. The Lord spoke to me about moving our family to southern California where our television studio and media ministry are located. When I shared this with Suzanne, she said, "Well, if this is important, the Lord will speak to *both* of us."

In the summer of 1999, God's direction became crystal clear to both Suzanne and me—the lights had turned green! Our family made the move to California and we announced that the headquarters of the healing ministry was relocating to Dallas.

THE RIGHT DECISION

I wish you could have attended the meeting of our board of directors as we discussed what was about to transpire. I have never seen such a burst of excitement and creativity. There was also a mighty presence of the Lord as we recommitted ourselves to reaching the world for Christ. It was obvious that to accomplish what God has called us to do, this was the right decision.

Our accountants, after considerable analysis, concluded, "This is good stewardship. The relocation to Dallas will save millions of dollars over the next few years."

This central U.S. location, with its major airport, will cut travel costs dramatically and make the world more accessible for our people. Also, the Metroplex area has the resources we need to expand our outreach and utilize current technology to touch lost and hurting people around the globe.

For quite some time we had been using the services of a major accounting firm in Dallas. Now, their in-house audits will be only a short drive rather than involving expensive flights and housing. In addition, the firm we use for legal representation is headquartered in Dallas.

We are embarking on the second quarter-century of ministry with a vision wider than any ocean. Plans are underway for a World Healing Center and International Partner Headquarters. It is designed in an old-world architectural style and finished with a stone foundation similar to those found in the Holy Land. It will truly be a beautiful setting that will inspire all who come to visit—a place of hope and healing.

The World Healing Center and International Partner Headquarters will include:

The *Healing Gardens*—a place of special beauty and tranquillity where faith can be strengthened amid a lush setting of trees, plants, pools, and streams. As you walk the garden paths, you will hear biblical accounts of the miracles from the Old and New Testaments at special locations where life-size bronze statues will depict those events.

The *Healing Stream*—flowing throughout the gardens and representing the healing stream that flows from our Lord. This will be a lovely brook that originates at the Healing Fountain. As it winds through the gardens there will be several places to sit and enjoy the presence of the Lord.

The *Healing Fountain*—an area where people will be reminded, through Scriptures inscribed at every fountainhead, of the miracle-working power of God.

The *People's Healing Cathedral*—the spire atop the roof, the stone exterior and stained-glass windows will all help create an unforgettable setting for the special services to be held there. The auditorium and interior will resemble a great cathedral you would see in Europe. In addition, there will be special prayer and healing booths in private areas of the cathedral designed for personal ministry.

The International Partner Center—where visitors will be able to see the many different outreaches of the ministry. There will be viewing screens around the interior and, with the use of audio-visual media, people can see and "be a part of" crusade services and international outreaches.

The *Hall of Faith*—where we will honor miracle ministries and evangelists of the past and present. This will be a living legacy to the healing power of God and the great men and women who have answered His call. There will also be a chapel with animation that will minister especially to children.

The *Healing Prayer Tower*—a place where prayer will be offered up twenty-four hours a day, seven days a week. This outreach will extend God's saving and healing power to people who will phone or visit from around the world.

The *Eternal Healing Flame*—will be lit twenty-four hours a day, 365 days a year, reminding us that the miracle-working power of God is always available.

In addition, there will be an outdoor amphitheater for special events, a Healing Library, and much more.

The World Healing Center and International Partner Headquarters is going to be a memorable place, anointed of the Lord to touch lives around the world. It is the central point of our ministry and will be visited by thousands of partners and visitors from many nations.

Everything we have planned for this property has one purpose in mind—to let the world know there is still One in heaven who declares, "I am the LORD who heals you" (Ex. 15:26) and that "Jesus Christ is the same yesterday, today, and forever" (Heb. 13:8).

The new center will complement the television production facilities in California and our ministry offices in Canada, Great Britain, Australia, and other nations.

Most important, the limits have been removed from our growth. Just as I felt I was in God's perfect will by establishing a church in Orlando in the early 1980s, I feel that same assurance as we embark on this new venture. I will be forever grateful to the congregation and the staff of World Outreach Church— known for many years as Orlando Christian Center. Their love toward me and my family was without limits, and I thank God for the lives that were touched because we answered God's call.

Those of you who know this ministry understand that it involves dozens of projects in many different locations, yet it all stems from one calling—*to take the saving and healing message of the gospel to every nation of the earth.*

WHAT A JOURNEY!

There have been many special moments in this quarter-century of miracles—and I have received more honors than I deserve. However, none have more meaning than something that was said to me one night in a little second-story apartment in Ramallah, Israel—across the street from where my late grandfather had his candy and sandwich shop.

My dear Armenian grandmother, Amal, before she passed from this life, was seated beside me on the couch of her humble home. Several of my cousins were gathered around. This elderly woman, who for so many years had found it impossible to understand my spiritual conversion, placed her time-worn hands over mine and quietly said, "Benny, now you are the patriarch of our family."

Those are words I will always revere. It is also a responsibility I do not take lightly.

I had no idea of the drastic transformation that was about to occur when I walked into that student-led prayer meeting at Georges Vanier Secondary School in Toronto so many years ago. What a journey it has been!

Twenty-five years ago, December 7, 1974, I stood on the platform of a small church in Oshawa, Ontario. That night, God touched me. He loosened my stammering tongue and I have never stopped telling the world about the God of love and miracles I serve.

Last week as I once again stood on a crusade platform, my eyes were filled with tears as I considered how far God has brought me. From the depths of my heart, I sang:

> He touched me,
> Oh, He touched me.
> And Oh, the joy that floods my soul.
> Something happened, and now I know.
> He touched me, and made me whole.*

This is not the end of the story. I pray that if the Lord tarries, the next twenty-five years will be greater than anything I have

---

* "He Touched Me" words and music by William J. Gaither. Copyright © 1963 William J. Gaither, Inc. All rights controlled by Gaither Copyright Management. Used by permission.

ever imagined—"Now to Him who is able to do exceedingly abundantly above all that we ask or think, according to the power that works in us" (Eph. 3:20). And I pray my life will always glorify my wonderful Lord and Master, Jesus Christ, the Son of the living God. Amen!